GLORIOUS HEAVEN

JESUS LOVES YOU
AND IS EXPECTING YOU

NICK REECE

I dedicate this book to my Savior Jesus Christ. Lord Jesus use this book for Your glory and save as many people as you can. Bring people to Heaven Lord Jesus. May people get saved who read this book so that they can spend eternity with you Jesus Christ in Heaven. I also dedicate this book to my grandfather who is in Heaven now. I can wait to see you again in Heaven. Heaven will truly be glorious when we are reunited once again in Heaven.

Acknowledgements

To my friend Branden Garcia who is a true brother in Christ to me. Your friendship means so much to me. Thank you for your friendship. Branden you have many heavenly rewards waiting for you in Heaven. Jesus Christ loves you so much.

To my mother Christy Cox who is a strong godly woman. Your devotion towards Jesus Christ is noticed by Jesus and His angels. Thank you for your love and support towards me. Jesus will reward you greatly Mom.

To my sister Stephanie Cox who has a passionate heart to sing for Jesus Christ on her guitar. When you sing on your guitar to Jesus Christ the angels sing with you.

To my grandmother Katherine Medina who always has a servant's heart to serve people with a joyful spirit. Thank you for all the times you cook for our family. Jesus will reward you for your hospitality.

To my father Aaron Cox who is a hard worker. Jesus loves you so much and Jesus takes notice of your work. Jesus will reward you for your devotion to Him.

Contents

Chapter 1

How can we know that we are going to Heaven?

Before we can talk about the wonders and pleasures of Heaven. I thought it would be wise to first explain how you can know you're going to Heaven. Let's say a young man is offered a plane ticket by an elderly woman to an amazing country like Italy. But there is a problem the young man has no idea how to get to the airport because the elderly woman never told him how to get there. So if the young man doesn't know how to get to the airport then no matter how many times the young man hears about how wonderful Italy is; he won't be able to get there himself. It is the same thing when someone is explaining the rewards, pleasures, joys, excitement, and happiness of Heaven. Sure you can talk to that person about all those great things about Heaven. But if they do not know Jesus and are not covered by Jesus Christ's blood for the full forgiveness of their sins then they will never experience Heaven.

So whoever is reading this I would like to present the Gospel to you. You see in the beginning God created Adam and Eve the first two human beings that ever walked upon the Earth. God planted a garden called Eden and Adam and Eve could eat from almost every tree except for one. The tree which God told them that they could not eat from was the tree of the knowledge of good and evil. Then Satan entered a serpent which was in the garden and deceived Eve into eating from the tree of the knowledge of good and evil. Adam also sinned and ate from the fruit which Eve ate. Because of Adam and Eve's disobedience to God sin entered the world. It brought spiritual death but also physical death.

Then God cursed the ground because Adam listened to Eve and ate from the tree of knowledge of good and evil. God also pronounced a punishment for Eve which was painful childbirth. Because Adam and Eve sinned they were separated from God. And from that point on all of humanity became sinners and have a fallen sin nature. Men, women, and children are all sinners. Everyone is a sinner. In the book of Isaiah it talks about how our sins separate us from God. Here is the verse.

(Isaiah 59:2 KJV)

2. But your iniquities have separated between you and your God, and your sins have hid his face from you, that he will not hear.

Because our sins have separated us from God when we die we would go to Hell. We would spend an eternity in Hell where we would be in agonizing pain in the flame of fire and we would also be living in terrifying eternal darkness. Sinners cannot earn their way to Heaven. We have an eternal problem and we cannot fix it ourselves. This eternal problem is something only God can fix. Now let's get back to what God says to the serpent in the garden of Eden.

God says a curse to the serpent but also a future promise concerning what He would do to the serpent. Here is the verse.

(Genesis 3:14-15 KJV)

14. And the LORD God said unto the serpent, Because thou hast done this, thou art cursed above all cattle, and above every beast of the field; upon thy belly shalt thou go, and dust shalt thou eat all the days of thy life: 15. And I will put enmity between thee and the woman, and between thy seed and her seed; it shall bruise thy head, and thou shalt bruise his heel.

Now the seed which God spoke about was Jesus Christ. Jesus was the Promise. Jesus was God's answer to our eternal problem of sin. Jesus is the only way we can escape the condemnation of Hell. The serpent was Satan and when God said the serpent shall bruise His heel. God was speaking about when Satan killed Jesus by crucifying Him on the Cross. But three days later Jesus rose from the dead defeating Sin, Satan, Hell, and Death. Here are some verses that describe what happened on the Cross.

(Colossians 2:14-15 KJV)

14. Blotting out the handwriting of ordinances that was against us, which was contrary to us, and took it out of the way, nailing it to his cross; 15. And having spoiled principalities and powers he made a shew of them openly, triumphing over them in it.

Our sins were nailed to the Cross as Jesus was nailed to the Cross. When it speaks of principalities and powers it is speaking of Satan and the fallen angels. Jesus defeated Satan and the fallen angels at the Cross. Jesus triumphed over Satan. Here is another verse that talks about what Jesus did to Satan at the Cross. I like this verse because it speaks about the fear of death. Which many of us are afraid to die. I hope this verse encourages you.

(Hebrews 2:14-15 KJV)

14. Forasmuch then as the children are partakers of flesh and blood, he also himself likewise took part of the same; that through death he might destroy him that had the power of death, that is, the devil; 15. And deliver them who through fear of death were all their lifetime subject to bondage.

When God said to the serpent it shall bruise thy head. God was speaking about this very thing that Jesus did to Satan at the Cross. Because of Jesus Christ's death on the cross Jesus took away from the Devil; Satan's power over death. Jesus's death on the cross also took away the fear of death. Now all those who are saved and are going to Heaven no longer have to fear death. We must choose Jesus Christ before we die. There are no second chances of choosing Jesus after we die. People in Hell cannot choose Jesus to save them. For them it is too late. That's why it's so important to choose Jesus today. Only Jesus can save us. Here is a Bible verse to prove my point that only Jesus can save us from Hell.

(Acts 4:10-12 KJV)

10. Be it known unto you all, and to all the people of Israel, that by the name of Jesus Christ of Nazareth, whom ye crucified, whom God raised from the dead, even by him doth this man stand here before you whole. 11. This is the stone which was set at nought of you builders, which is become the head of the corner. 12. Neither is there salvation in any other: for there is none other name under heaven given among men, whereby we must be saved.

Jesus is the only name and the only person who can save us from Hell. Our good works can't save us. Our church can't save us. The pastor can't save us. No other false religion or false prophet can save us. Here is another verse that further explains the exclusivity of going to Heaven. Jesus said He was the only way for us to get to Heaven. Here is the verse.

(John 14:6 KJV)

6. Jesus saith unto him, I am the way, the truth, and the life: no man cometh unto the Father, but by me.

Notice that Jesus did not say I am a way. He did not say I am one of the ways. He said I am the way. And when Jesus said no man cometh unto the Father but by me. Jesus was saying that God the Father lives in Heaven and the only way people can get to Heaven and see God the Father in Heaven is through Jesus Christ. Here are some verses to explain why it is so important to choose Jesus today.

(Hebrews 9:27 KJV)

27. And as it is appointed unto men once to die,
but after this the judgment:

(2 Corinthians 6:2 KJV)

2. (For he saith, I have heard thee in a time accepted, and in the
day of salvation have I succoured thee: behold now is the
accepted time; behold now is the day of salvation.)

(Revelation 20:14-15 KJV)

14. And death and hell were cast into the lake of fire. This is the
second death. 15. And whosover was not found written in the
book of life was cast into the lake of fire.

The Book of Life is a book containing the names of people who are saved and are going to Heaven. These people will be allowed to enter Heaven and live there forever. The only way you can get your name written in the Book of Life and not go to the lake of fire is to believe in Jesus Christ, repent of your sins, and ask Jesus to forgive you of your sins. Immediately after you choose to believe in Jesus then your name will be written in the Book of Life.

God loves you so much that He did not want to spend an eternity separated from you. God wants to save us from Hell and that is why God sent Jesus Christ to pay the penalty for our sins. Jesus Christ died for you personally as he hung on the Cross. He thought about you and how much He loved you as He was dying on the cross. God chose to have Jesus come into the world through a virgin named Mary. An angel named Gabriel comes to Mary and says she shall give birth to a Son and she shall call his name Jesus. Mary is confused because she had never been with a man. Here are the verses that talk about how Jesus would be born.

(Luke 1:30-35 KJV)

30. And the angel said unto her, Fear not, Mary for thou hast found favour with God. 31. And behold, thou shalt conceive in thy womb, and bring forth a son, and shalt call his name Jesus. 32. He shall be great, and shall be called the Son of the Highest: and the Lord God shall give unto him the throne of his father David: 33. And he shall reign over the house of Jacob forever; and of his kingdom there shall be no end. 34. Then said Mary unto the angel, How shall this be, seeing I know not a man? 35. And the angel answered and said unto her, The Holy Ghost shall come upon thee, and the power of the Highest shall overshadow thee: therefore also that holy thing which shall be born of thee shall be called the Son of God.

Here is another verse which shows the power of Jesus Christ and that only He can save people from their sins. No one else can save you from your sins except Jesus Christ. In other words there is no one who can forgive you of your sins completely and eternally except Jesus Christ. You cannot earn your forgiveness of sins no matter what you do. It is only by accepting Jesus' sacrifice and what He did for you on the cross when He shed His own blood for you that you will be forgiven. This verse was spoken about Jesus before He was born. Here is the verse.

(Matthew 1:20-21 KJV)

20. But while he thought on these things, behold, the angel of the LORD appeared unto him in a dream, saying, Joseph, thou son of David, fear not to take unto thee Mary thy wife: for that which is conceived in her is of the Holy Ghost. 21. And she shall bring forth a son, and thou shalt call his name JESUS: for he shall save his people from their sins.

Jesus has the ability, the power, the authority, and He has a desire to forgive people of their sins. Jesus loves to forgive people and show them mercy and grace. It is by the gift of God through His grace that He allows us to be saved and go to Heaven. No good works that we have done could ever save us. It is purely and completely by grace through faith in Jesus Christ that anyone is saved. Here is the verse to explain this point more clearly.

(Ephesians 2:8-9 KJV)

8. For by grace are ye saved through faith; and that not of yourselves: it is the gift of God: 9. Not of works, lest any man should boast.

There are three people in the Triune Godhead. There is God the Father, God the Son, and God the Holy Spirit. Each of them have different parts that they do. All three of them are equally God. God the Father is God. God the Son is Jesus Christ who is also God. God the Holy Spirit is God. Jesus grew up and became a man. He was then crucified and He took the sins of the whole world of everyone who has ever lived or will live upon Himself. Now there is a reason Jesus had to die and be crucified. It was because Jesus is God so only He could pay for our sins. We couldn't get to Heaven on our own because we are all sinners. And God hates sin. Jesus' blood was perfect it was the blood of God. It was God's blood that was gushing out of Jesus. Because it was God's blood God the Father could look at Jesus' death and accept the payment of our sins because there was perfect blood which paid the full payment of sins. Here is a verse that talk about Jesus's blood paying for our sins.

(Matthew 26:26-28 KJV)

26. And as they were eating, Jesus took bread, and blessed it, and brake it, and gave it to the disciples, and said, Take, eat; this is my body. 27. And he took the cup, and gave thanks, and gave it to them saying, Drink ye all of it; 28. For this is my blood of the new testament, which is shed for many for the remission of sins.

The word remission means forgiveness of sins. Because of Jesus' blood which He shed for us we can now be forgiven.You see as we accept Jesus Christ. Jesus at that moment forgives us eternally. Jesus forgives us of our past sins, our present sins, and our future sins. But wait there is more to the gospel message. Jesus died on a cross and was buried but three days later Jesus rose from the dead. Jesus rose from the dead to prove He was God but also to show that God accepted Jesus's sacrifice when He shed His blood on the cross to pay for our sins. Here is a verse to make the gospel message more plainly. You probably know the verse that I am going to say.

(John 3:16 KJV)

16. For God so loved the world, that he gave his only begotten Son, that whosoever believeth in him should not perish but have everlasting life.

So basically the gospel message is we sinned against God and we couldn't do anything to fix it. But God sent His Son Jesus to die on a cross to pay for our sins with His blood. Three days later He rose from the dead. If we believe in Jesus Christ and repent of our sins we shall receive eternal life which is Heaven and we shall not perish which is Hell. Here is the Romans Road that will explain the gospel with more clarity. It is what we Christians call the gospel message in the book of Romans.

(Romans 3:10-12 and 23 KJV)

10. As it is written, There is none righteous, no not one: 11. There is none that understandeth, there is none that seeketh after God. 12. They are all gone out of the way, they are together become unprofitable; there is none that doeth good, no, not one. 23. For all have sinned, and come short of the glory of God;

(Romans 6:23 KJV)

23. For the wages of sin is death; but the gift of God is eternal life through Jesus Christ our Lord.

(Romans 5:8 KJV)

8. But God commendeth his love toward us, in that, while we were yet sinners, Christ died for us.

(Romans 10:9-11 and 13 KJV)

9. That if thou shalt confess with thy mouth the Lord Jesus, and shalt believe in thine heart that God hath raised him from the dead, thou shalt be saved. 10. For with the heart man believeth unto righteousness; and with the mouth confession is made unto salvation. 11. For the scripture saith, Whosoever believeth on him shall not be ashamed.

13. For whosoever shall call upon the name of the Lord shall be saved.

(Romans 5:1 KJV)

1. Therefore being justified by faith, we have peace with God through our Lord Jesus Christ:

(Romans 8:1 KJV)

1. There is therefore now no condemnation to them which are in Christ Jesus, who walk not after the flesh, but after the Spirit.

If you put your faith in Jesus Christ and repent of your sins then you are going to Heaven. The reason we can go to Heaven is because Jesus made peace with God by dying on the cross and shedding His blood for our sins. Jesus took all of our sinfulness, guilt, shame, and regret and put it on Himself when He was on the cross. In exchange for our sinfulness Jesus gave us His Righteousness. So whenever God looks at us; we who are Christians who have been covered by Jesus' blood; all God sees is Jesus' Righteousness. I would be doing you an injustice if I did not give you the verse which Jesus talks about the way we should live our lives. Here is the verse.

(Matthew 7:13-14 KJV)

13. Enter ye in at the strait gate: for wide is the gate, and broad is the way, that leadeth to destruction, and many there be which go in thereat: 14. Because strait is the gate, and narrow is the way, which leadeth unto life, and few there be that find it.

If you want to get off the broad road that leads to Destruction and Hell and get on the narrow road which leads to life and Heaven. You must accept Jesus Christ as your Lord and Savior. You must repent of your sins and ask Jesus to forgive you of your sins. Then start living for Jesus. Being a Christian is not easy. As a Christian and believer in Jesus Christ you will have many temptations coming your way. The Devil will always try to get you back on the broad road to Hell. The Devil will place temptations in front of you. The Devil wants you to fail. But Jesus will always help you stay on the narrow road to Heaven. Jesus wants you to succeed in your journey towards Heaven. As you say no to each temptation that comes your way. You will be staying on the narrow road to Heaven. Many people have left the narrow road to Heaven and gone back on the highway to Hell because it is easier for them to sin than to live a righteous life for Jesus Christ. May that never be said of you and me.

I have a verse that has helped me tremendously with my walk with Christ. For years I have always struggled with knowing whether I was saved or not. For my brothers and sisters in Christ around the world this verse is for you personally. If you believe in Jesus Christ and have repented of your sins then God says you have eternal life and that you will go to Heaven after you die. Repenting of sins is turning away from your sins. If your sin is lying then stop lying and start to tell the truth. If your sin is stealing then stop stealing and get a job and work hard for your money so that way you don't have to steal. That way you can buy your own stuff.

If your sin is lust then stop lusting and focus on how God views the sacredness of sex and marriage. Focus on Bible Scriptures that help you think righteous and holy thoughts and not sinful and lustful thoughts. I hope this verse encourages you my fellow brothers and sisters in Christ who may be struggling with your salvation. Know that God's Word is truth. This Bible verse below is God's true words about how to know for sure you are saved and are going to Heaven.

(1 John 5:13 KJV)

13. These things have I written unto you that believe on the name of the Son of God; that ye may know that ye have eternal life, and that ye may believe on the name of the Son of God.

Jesus Christ is also called the Son of God. If you believe in Jesus Christ you can know for sure that you have eternal life and are going to Heaven. You will be in Heaven with Jesus for eternity. And that is eternal life.

Chapter 2

Storing up Treasures in Heaven!

Now that we have talked about how to get to Heaven; we should talk about storing up treasures in Heaven. Some people think it is dumb to store up treasures in Heaven because they can't enjoy it now on the Earth. But that is because some people don't realize it is smarter to store up treasures in Heaven than to store up treasures on Earth. They forget that treasures on the Earth are temporary but treasures in Heaven are eternal. Let's see what Jesus had to say on this matter of treasures.

(Matthew 6:19-21 KJV)

19. Lay not up for yourselves treasures upon earth, where moth and rust doth corrupt, and where thieves break through and steal: 20. But lay up for yourselves treasures in heaven, where neither moth nor rust doth corrupt, and where thieves do not break through nor steal: 21. For where your treasure is, there will your heart be also.

The treasures on Earth will be lost, stolen, and will not last forever. One day you will die and leave all your treasures on Earth for someone else to have. All of your hard work would have been for nothing. But if your treasures are in Heaven then when you die you will go to your treasures and you'll be immensely blessed. So the question you should be asking is how do you store up treasures in Heaven? I hope these verses will encourage you and give you new insight into how you can store up treasures in Heaven.

(Matthew 19:21 KJV)

21. Jesus said unto him, If thou wilt be perfect, go and sell that thou hast, and give to the poor, and thou shalt have treasure in heaven: and come and follow me.

(Luke 12:33 KJV)

33. Sell that ye have, and give alms; provide yourselves bags which wax not old, a treasure in the heavens that faileth not, where no thief approacheth, neither moth corrupteth.

(Luke 18:22 KJV)

22. Now when Jesus heard these things, he said unto him, Yet lackest thou one thing: sell all that thou hast, and distribute unto the poor, and thou shalt have treasure in heaven: and come, follow me.

(1 Timothy 6:17-19 KJV)

17. Charge them that are rich in this world, that they be not highminded, nor trust in uncertain riches, but in the living God, who giveth us richly all things to enjoy; 18. That they do good, that they be rich in good works, ready to distribute, willing to communicate; 19. Laying up in store for themselves a good foundation against the time to come, that they may lay hold on eternal life.

(Matthew 25:34-40 KJV)

34. Then shall the King say unto them on his right hand, Come, ye blessed of my Father, inherit the kingdom prepared for you from the foundation of the world: 35. For I was hungred, and ye gave me meat: I was thirsty, and ye gave me drink: I was a stranger, and ye took me in: 36. Naked, and ye clothed me: I was sick, and ye visited me: I was in prison, and ye came unto me. 37. Then

shall the righteous answer him, saying, Lord, when saw we thee
and hungred, and fed thee? or thirsty, and gave thee drink? 38.
When saw we thee a stranger, and took thee in? or naked, and
clothed thee? 39. Or when saw we thee sick, or in prison, and
came unto thee? 40. And the King shall answer and say unto
them, Verily I say unto you, Inasmuch as ye have done it unto
one of the least of these my brethren, ye have done it unto me.

When you give money to someone who is poor, when you give
someone clothes, when you give someone food, when you give
someone something to drink, when you visit the sick, and when
you visit people in prison you are actually doing it for Jesus. Jesus
is the King of kings. Jesus is the King which is being spoken of in
this portion of Scripture. Here are some other verses about giving
and treasures in Heaven.

(Matthew 10:42 KJV)

42. And whosover shall give to drink unto one of these little ones
a cup of cold water only in the name of a disciple, verily I say
unto you, he shall in no wise lose his reward.

(Proverbs 19:17 KJV)

17. He that hath pity upon the poor lendeth unto the Lord;
and that which he hath given will he pay him again.

(Luke 16:9 KJV)

9. And I say unto you, Make to yourselves friends of the
mammon of unrighteousness; that, when ye fail,
they may receive you into everlasting habitations.

Most of the ways that we store up treasures in Heaven is by using
our money to help people in need. As you can see in the verses
above it talks about giving to the poor. When it speaks about
mammon of unrigtheousness in Luke 16:9 it is just talking about

the money we use here on Earth. Money can be used for unrighteous purposes which is why Jesus calls it unrighteous mammon or unrighteous money. We are supposed to give to people in need; and our treasure in Heaven for Luke 16:9 is we will be welcomed into other people's homes in Heaven. Imagine having dinner in Heaven with your best friend in their heavenly mansion. Think about being invited to someone's mansion in Heaven just because you gave to them when you were on Earth. Because we give to people who need our help; one day in Heaven they shall thank us for our giving to them. They shall talk about the kind of impact that our giving had on them.

Also whenever we give to the poor we are giving to the Lord and the Lord says He will repay us. People think that when they give their money away to the poor that they will never get it back. They don't understand that Jesus will pay them back in Heaven. Giving money away to the poor is not a sacrifice but an investment for our treasure in Heaven. Jesus Himself said that when we give our money to the poor or more specifically to someone who cannot pay us back; that we will be rewarded in Heaven. Here are some verses that talk about money and being repayed back in Heaven. This verse is Jesus Himself speaking.

(Luke 14:12-14 KJV)

12. Then said he also to him that bade him, When thou makest a dinner or a supper, call not thy friends, nor thy brethren, neither thy kinsmen, nor thy rich neighbours; lest they also bid thee again, and a recompense be made thee. 13. But when thou makest a feast, call the poor, the maimed, the lame, the blind: 14. And thou shalt be blessed; for they cannot recompense thee: for thou shalt be recompensed at the resurrection of the just.

The word recompensed means that it will be paid back. So the verse could say that you shall be repaid at the resurrection of the just. That is a very good thing. When it says the resurrection of the just that means when we are in Heaven. This next verse is the apostle Paul speaking to the Philippian church about how their generous giving to Paul is being deposited into their heavenly account. That is so cool. Paul was in need and the Philippian church financially supported him whenever they could. So remember to be generous with your money as you give to people. You want your bank account in Heaven to be huge.

(Philippians 4:16-17 KJV)

16. For even in Thessalonica ye sent once and again unto my necessity. 17. Not because I desire a gift: but I desire fruit that may abound to your account.

(2 Corinthians 9:6-7 KJV)

6. But this I say, He which soweth sparingly shall reap also sparingly; and he which soweth bountifully shall reap also bountifully. 7. Every man according as he purposeth in his heart, so let him give; not grudgingly, or of necessity: for God loveth a cheerful giver.

When it talks about us giving without grudgingly; it is not talking about our tithe to God. The giving it is talking about is our freewill offerings or our freewill giving. The giving it is focusing on is the money we give beyond the tithe. First we give our tithe to God in obedience. But after we have given our tithe; then we get the honor and priviledge to think of ways to bless people with our giving. Do you see the love of God in 2 Corinthians 9:7? *As he purposeth in his heart, so let him give; not grudgingly, or of necessity: for God loveth a cheerful giver.* God allows us to decide how much money we want to give to people. God loves it when we give to people. It puts a smile on Jesus Christ's face when we give. People sometimes say God loves a cheerful giver and since they are not cheerful when they give that means that they don't have to give. Giving takes practice. The more you give the easier it becomes. After a while you will enjoy giving and you will become a cheerful giver.

I would suggest that if you are not giving to your local church. That you should start by giving to your church the first 10 percent of each paycheck you get. The first ten percent of each paycheck you get goes to God. That is considered your tithe to God. Don't spend all your money on bills and then give God what is left over. God does not want your leftovers. He wants the best you can give Him. He wants the fresh meal not the stale, and soggy leftovers.

God's Word says that if you give generously then you will be paid back generously. That is what it means when it says he which so-weth bountifully shall reap also bountifully. Let this verse encourage you my brothers and sisters in Christ who give to the Lord faithfully. God is watching and will reward you in Heaven. In the verse below Jesus tells us what He will give us for those who have left all to follow Him. Those who give their time for Jesus and the gospel, those who give their money for Jesus, and those who use their talents for Jesus. Jesus will reward everyone who has lived their lives for the purpose of Jesus Christ and the gospel.

(Mark 10:28-31 KJV)

28. Then Peter began to say unto him, Lo, we have left all, and have followed thee. 29. And Jesus answered and said, Verily I say unto you, There is no man that hath left house, or brethren, or sisters, or father, or mother, or wife, or children, or lands, for my sake, and the gospel's, 30. But he shall receive an hundredfold now in this time, houses, and brethren, and sisters, and mothers, and children, and lands, with persecutions; and in the world to come eternal life. 31. But many that are first shall be last; and the last first.

Every person who has lived their life for Jesus will be rewarded beyond their wildest dreams in Heaven. Take comfort in the fact that this Earth is not all there is. Heaven is our true home. I would like to end this chapter with a final verse that Jesus Christ said when He was talking about giving. Here is the verse.

(Acts 20:35 KJV)

35. I have shewed you all things, how that so labouring ye ought to support the weak, and to remember the words of the Lord Jesus, how he said, It is more blessed to give than to receive.

It's a joy to give. When I give I become happy. Do you ever get that good feeling in your heart after you've given to someone? That means that Jesus told the truth when He said it is more blessed to give than to receive. Jesus always tells the truth because He is Truth. Giving does not save you; but giving shows that there has been a change in your heart. You are more generous with your money. Your heart breaks when you see someone in need. Because of the change in your heart you give them money because you care about them. You want to show your love to God by giving to His people. Just like how God gave you His Son Jesus Christ. I hope these verses are showing you how important it is to give to people in need. It is for their benefit but also for your benefit. Giving is a way to store up treasures in Heaven. Sure you can give away your time, and talents but Scripture mostly talks about giving away your money to people in need as a way to store up treasures in Heaven. You can't take your money with you when you die on Earth. But you can send your money on ahead to Heaven in the form of heavenly treasures.

CHAPTER 3

CROWNS IN HEAVEN!

Since we have talked about storing up treasures in Heaven. Let's talk about the crowns which faithful believers of Christ will receive in Heaven. I love crowns. Crowns are a symbol of royalty. It also shows authority. We shall talk about five crowns which the Bible talks about. I believe that each individual crown a believer receives in Heaven will come with a position of authority. God will give that believer in Christ a God given position of authority. Now we shall talk about the crowns.

The first crown is called the Incorruptible Crown. Here is the verse which mentions the Incorruptible Crown in Scripture.

(1 Corinthians 9:24-25 KJV)

24. Know ye not that they which run in a race run all, but one receiveth the prize? So run, that ye may obtain. 25. And every man that striveth for the mastery is temperate in all things. Now they do it to obtain a corruptible crown; but we an incorruptible.

Now the word temperate means to self restrain. As an athlete they restrain themselves from indulging in unwise things. An athlete stops himself from eating a ten pound cake; because he knows that if he eats it that he will feel heavy and lose the race. He will not get the prize. The apostle Paul makes an illustration of the Christian life as an athletic competition. So it would suggest that one receives the Incorruptible Crown by denying oneself. Now you may be asking but how do I deny myself; I keep giving into my sinful desires? The only way you can deny yourself is through the power of the Holy Spirit. I believe the reason we choose to sin is because we have lost the perspective of God's goodness to us. We have forgotten how good God really is. Here is a verse explaining the goodness of God.

(Psalm 27:13-14 KJV)

13. I had fainted, unless I had believed to see the goodness of the LORD in the land of the living. 14. Wait on the LORD: be of good courage, and he shall strengthen thine heart:
wait, I say, on the LORD.

This verse was written by a man named King David in ancient times. David had a tough, long, and difficult life. When he was younger he was chased by King Saul who tried to kill David. Then later in David's life David's son Absalom tried to take the throne and kill David. Needless to say it is easy to understand why David almost went to despair. But the thing that kept David going through life was that one day He would see the goodness of the Lord while he was still alive on Earth. David was leaning on on the Lord to give him strength in his heart. The Lord's strength would help David get through each day.

David did see the goodness of the Lord while he was still alive on Earth. God made a promise to David that through David's lineage would come the Messiah. God also promised that the Messiah would have a kingdom that would last forever. The Messiah was Jesus Christ. Jesus Christ was the promise. You see if we forget about the goodness of God; then that will lead us to despair. Which will eventually lead us to sin against God. Here are some verses that explain how you can overcome your fleshly desires by follow-ing the Holy Spirit.

(Romans 8:5-6 KJV)

5. For they that are after the flesh do mind the things of the flesh; but they that are after the Spirit the things of the Spirit. 6. For to be carnally minded is death; but to be spiritually minded is life and peace.

(Galatians 5:16-17 KJV)

16. This I say then, Walk in the Spirit, and ye shall not fulfill the lust of the flesh. 17. For the flesh lusteth against the Spirit, and the Spirit against the flesh: and these are contrary the one to the other: so that ye cannot do the things that ye would.

You see if you keep focusing on the things of this world. Like if you are constantly looking at pornography. Or if you are always drunk. If you eat more food than what you need to eat. Those things are the lusts of the flesh. Now the things of the Holy Spirit would be self control, love, patience, joy, peace, goodness. There are things that you can do to be more filled with the Holy Spirit. Stuff like praying, reading your Bible, resisting temptation, memorizing Scripture, and giving to the poor. You can also ask for the Holy Spirit. Jesus Himself told us that we can ask for the Holy Spirit. Here is the Bible verse.

(Luke 11:13 KJV)

13. If ye then, being evil, know how to give good gifts unto your children: how much more shall your heavenly Father give the Holy Spirit to them that ask him?

I have one final bible verse to encourage you to die to self and live for Jesus Christ. This verse puts everything into perspective which helps us focus on eternity instead of focusing on the temporary. Here is the verse.

(Matthew 16:24-27 KJV)

24. Then said Jesus unto his disciples, If any man will come after me, let him deny himself, and take up his cross, and follow me. 25. For whosoever will save his life shall lose it: and whosoever will lose his life for my sake shall find it. 26. For what is a man profited, if he shall gain the whole world, and lose his own soul? or what shall a man give in exchange for his soul? 27. For the Son of man shall come in the glory of his Father with his angels; and then he shall reward every man according to his works.

You see if you gave into your sinful desires and somehow you gained the whole world which is only temporary; but in the process you lost your soul for eternity then that would not be a wise thing to do. Any man or woman would be considered a fool if they did that. Sadly that is happening to many people. Deny yourself and follow Jesus. As you deny yourself for Jesus you are losing your life. But in the end you will find your life in Heaven when Jesus rewards you with the Incorruptible Crown. Focus on the prize of the Incorruptible Crown. You'll be glad you did it.

The second crown we shall talk about is the Crown of Rejoicing. Here is the verse which mentions the Crown of Rejoicing.

(1 Thessalonians 2:19-20 KJV)

19. For what is our hope, or joy, or crown of rejoicing? Are not even ye in the presence of our Lord Jesus Christ at his coming? 20. For ye are our glory and joy.

The Crown of Rejoicing is for believers who lead other people to Jesus Christ. In other words this crown is for people who explain the gospel to people. Every time you witness to people and try to explain the gospel to them; Jesus takes notice. One day He will reward you for every time you shared the gospel with people in the form of the Crown of Rejoicing. Jesus desires to give you this crown because Jesus wants to show you that He is proud of you for not being ashamed of Him and telling people about Him. Do not give up in sharing the gospel with people because one day it will matter for eternity. Every time you share the gospel with people think about the day when you will receive the Crown of Rejoicing. Always share the gospel with people; you will be blessed for doing it. Jesus will reveal to you on that Day how your sharing the gospel with people affected them personally. I hope that you are deeply encouraged by that and that you will want to share your faith even more for the prize of the Crown of Rejoicing.

The third crown we shall talk about is the Crown of Life. Here are the verses that mention the Crown of Life.

(James 1:12 KJV)

12. Blessed is the man that endureth temptation: for when he is tried, he shall receive the crown of life, which the Lord hath promised to them that love him.

(Revelation 2:8-10 KJV)

8. And unto the angel of the church in Smyrna write; These things saith the first and the last, which was dead, and is alive; 9. I know thy works, and tribulation, and poverty, (but thou art rich) and I know the blasphemy of them which say they are Jews, and are not, but are the synagogue of Satan. 10. Fear none of those things which thou shalt suffer: behold, the devil shall cast some of you into prison, that ye may be tried; and ye shall have tribulation ten days: be faithful unto death, and I will give thee a crown of life.

The Crown of Life is for believers in Christ who resist temptation, and who remain faithful to Jesus Christ even if it means they are going to die. Now genuine believers in Jesus Christ who truly love Jesus will want to resist temptation because they love Jesus more than they love their sin. I love that Jesus Christ rewards us for resisting temptation. Jesus offers us the Crown of Life; what a wonderful reward for us. Now you may be asking yourself I really want the Crown of Life but I keep giving into temptation how do I stop giving into temptation? You are in luck the Bible offers us a solution. Here is the verse.

(1 Corinthians 10:13 KJV)

13. There hath no temptation taken you but such as is common to man: but God is faithful, who will not suffer you to be tempted above that ye are able; but will with the temptation also make a way to escape, that ye may be able to bear it.

Whenever you are tempted to sin just know that God has always made a way of escape. God has made a way to escape the temptation. If you are tempted to look at pornography then turn off the computer or even get rid of the computer. You don't want to miss out on the reward of the Crown of life just because you couldn't stop looking at pornography. The Crown of life is way better than pornography. Focus on the greater thing which is the Crown of life. Don't focus on the lesser thing which is pornography. Here is another way of saying it in the Bible.

(Colossians 3:1-2 KJV)

1. If ye then be risen with Christ, seek those things which are above, where Christ sitteth on the right hand of God. 2. Set your affection on things above, not on things on the earth.

(2 Corinthians 4:18 KJV)

18. While we look not at the things which are seen, but at the things which are not seen: for the things which are seen are temporal; but the things which are not seen are eternal.

When it says set your affection on things above in Colossians 3:1 it is speaking about Heaven. Our desire should be for heavenly things. We should desire and think about constantly things like heavenly rewards and the approval of Jesus Christ. And when it says the things which are seen in 2 Corinthians 4:18 it is speaking about the Earth. The things of this Earth are temporary but the things in Heaven are eternal. So to break this down for you. The Crown of Life is in Heaven and it is eternal. Pornography is on the

Earth but it is temporary. So there is one question you need to ask yourself. Are you going to live for something that is temporary (pornography)? Or are you going to live for something that is eternal (Crown of Life)?

There are many other temptations like stealing, lying, gluttony, and drunkness but those are just a few. Whatever your specific temptation is I would like for you to focus on the Crown of Life and for you to no longer give into your temptation. When you are tempted to sin think about the Crown of Life and the smile Jesus will have on His face as He places the Crown of Life on your head because you said no to your temptations. Also the Crown of Life is given to believers who die for their faith in Jesus Christ. Think about the countless Christians who have died for Jesus Christ. Those Christians gave their lives for Jesus because they loved Jesus more than they feared death. Those Christians who were murdered have a wonderful reward coming to them. That reward is the Crown of Life.

The fourth crown is called the Crown of Righteousness. Here is the verse which speaks about the Crown of Righteousness.

(2 Timothy 4:8 KJV)

8. Henceforth there is laid up for me a crown of righteousness, which the Lord, the righteous judge, shall give me at that day: and not to me only, but unto all them also that love his appearing.

The Crown of Righteousness is for believers who love Jesus and have longed for Jesus Christ's appearing. This is an amazing crown that we will receive from Jesus Christ. Those who are truly looking forward to Jesus Christ's appearing will no longer want to be in sin anymore. They will want to live righteously for Jesus so that they will not be ashamed when they see Jesus at His coming. We should abide in Jesus Christ so that we will have confidence when we see Him. Here is a verse that talks about seeing Jesus at His coming and how we should abide in Jesus.

(1 John 2:28 KJV)

28. And now, little children, abide in him; that,
when he shall appear, we may have confidence,
and not be ashamed before him at his coming.

Think about the day when Jesus Christ comes back for His Church. We call this the Rapture. Every Christian is considered the Church. So when Jesus comes back for His Church He is actually coming back for every genuine Christian. If you are a Christian you will see Jesus face to face. Don't you want to be happy when you see Jesus and not ashamed? If you want to be happy when you see Jesus then live for Jesus right now. Don't wait until the Rapture to change your life. Change your life right now. If you are stuck in sin then get godly people to help you overcome that sin. Make it your goal every day to please Jesus. Always keep in mind that Jesus is coming back for you and that you want Him to be proud of you when He sees you. Get rid of sin in your life and start to live righteously for Jesus Christ. Also here is a verse when Jesus told us about how we should abide in Him. I hope these verses will bring understanding to you and that you see how important it is to abide in Jesus Christ.

Here is the verse.

(John 15:1-10 KJV)

1. I am the true vine, and my Father is the husbandman. 2. Every branch in me that beareth not fruit he taketh away: and every branch that beareth fruit, he purgeth it, that it may bring forth more fruit. 3. Now ye are clean through the word which I have spoken unto you. 4. Abide in me, and I in you. As the branch cannot bear fruit of itself, except it abide in the vine; no more can ye, except ye abide in me. 5. I am the vine, ye are the branches: He that abideth in me, and I in him, the same bringeth forth much fruit: for without me ye can do nothing. 6. If a man abide not in me, he is cast forth as a branch, and is withered; and men gather them, and cast them into the fire, and they are burned. 7.

If ye abide in me, and my words abide in you, ye shall ask what
ye will, and it shall be done unto you. 8. Herein is my Father
glorified, that ye bear much fruit; so shall ye be my disciples. 9.
As the Father hath loved me, so have I loved you: continue ye in
my love. 10. If ye keep my commandments, ye shall abide in my
love; even as I have kept my Father's commandments,
and abide in his love.

When it says the word husbandman that just means like a farmer.
God the Father wants us to bear fruit like love, joy, peace, and
goodness. We can't bear fruit without abiding in Jesus Christ. If we
are continuosly doing sinful things, sinful thoughts, and sinful attitudes we are not abiding in Jesus Christ. But if we are doing
righteous things, changing our thoughts into godly thoughts, and
changing our attitudes into Christ like attitudes we are abiding in
Jesus Christ. Fruit could also be good works for other people. Good
works show that there has been a change in the person's heart.
Let's say you give money to someone in need. But before you came
to Jesus Christ you would not even give one penny to someone if
they asked you for money. That shows that there has been a
change in your heart. That is bearing fruit. Here is the verse that
talks about the fruit of the Holy Spirit.

(Galatians 5:22-23 KJV)

22. But the fruit of the Spirit is love, joy, peace, longsuffering,
gentleness, goodness, faith, 23. Meekness, temperance:
against such there is no law.

I hope you are getting excited for Heaven. Stuff like treasures,
crowns, rewards, and Jesus gets my imagination going. I am so excited for Heaven and I hope you are as well. Just love Jesus, live
righteously for Jesus, and keep looking forward to His appearing
and you shall receive the Crown of Righteousness.

The fifth crown is called the Crown of Glory. Here is the verse that
mentions the Crown of Glory in the Bible.

(1 Peter 5:2-4 KJV)

2. Feed the flock of God which is among you,
taking the oversight thereof, not by constraint, but willingly;
not for filthy lucre, but of a ready mind;
3. Neither as being lords over God's heritage,
but being examples to the flock.
4. And when the chief Shepherd shall appear,
ye shall receive a crown of glory that fadeth not away.

The Crown of Glory is for pastors who teach the Bible and care for believers in the church. Every time your pastor reads a Bible verse that someone desperately needed to hear; they are feeding the flock of God. Every time your pastor gives someone an encouraging word to make their day a little brighter they are making an eternal difference. This crown is mostly talking about how pastors should take care of their church congregations. The pastor of the church should be a godly example for his church members. One day pastors shall receive the Crown of Glory from the Chief Shepherd. The Chief Shepherd is Jesus Christ. The Lord Jesus Christ will honor the countless hours that pastors have spent in helping a fellow believer understand the Bible. What better reward for Jesus to give pastors for their devotion to help fellow believers learn the Word of God; then blessing them with a glorious crown called the Crown of Glory.

CHAPTER 4

REWARDS IN HEAVEN!

Now we come to even more exciting things. I'm talking about rewards in Heaven. Rewards are what Jesus gives us for our faithful service to Him. Our faithful service to Him could also be called our good works for Him and for His people. Rewards are not a bad thing to want. It is not selfish of you to want to be rewarded by Jesus. The reason it is not selfish for us to want to be rewarded; is because God was the One who put that desire in us in the first place. We like to be rewarded for our hard work. Here is a verse that speaks about the good food in the garden of Eden.

(Genesis 2:9 KJV)

9. And out of the ground made the LORD God to grow every tree that is pleasant to the sight, and good for food; the tree of life also in the midst of the garden, and the tree of knowledge of good and evil.

Here is a verse that talks about Adam working in the garden of Eden.

(Genesis 2:15 KJV)

15. And the LORD God took the man, and put him into the garden of Eden to dress it and to keep it.

Don't you think that Adam was looking forward to eating some good food from the trees in the garden of Eden; after a long day of working to keep the garden of Eden in good shape. The food was Adam's reward.

And who knows maybe when God walked and talked with Adam.

Perhaps God said to Adam, "Good job Adam. I love the way this garden looks. Keep up the good work."

Or let me make it closer to home. You work really hard at doing your job for what? Is it for Identity? Power? Respect? Or is it for something very simple like a paycheck? You work hard at your job because you want to be rewarded for your hard work in the form of a paycheck. You see there is nothing wrong for wanting to be rewarded for your work. Just like a student who studies for an up-coming test. What does the student hope to get from all of his studying? He hopes to be rewarded with a good grade on his test. The same thing goes for us wanting heavenly rewards after we have faithfully served Jesus with our entire lives. We desire to have authority. We desire to have satisfaction. We desire to have ownership. Jesus will completely fulfill these desires in us when we get to Heaven. We will be completely satisfied and our heart's desires will finally be realized and enjoyed in Heaven with Jesus.

Now we shall talk about the seven churches in the book of Revelation and the rewards that Jesus promises to the believers.

The Church of Ephesus is called the Loveless Church. Let's see what Jesus had to say to them. Here is the verse.

(Revelation 2:1-7 KJV)

1. Unto the angel of the church of Ephesus write; These things saith he that holdeth the seven stars in his right hand, who walketh in the midst of the seven gold candlesticks; 2. I know thy works, and thy labour, and thy patience, and how thou canst not bear them which are evil: and thou hast tried them which say they are apostles, and are not, and hast found them liars: 3. And hast borne, and hast patience, and for my name's sake hast laboured, and hast not fainted. 4. Nevertheless I have somewhat against thee, because thou hast left thy first love. 5. Remember therefore from whence thou art fallen, and repent, and do the first works; or else I will come unto thee quickly, and I will

remove thy candlestick out of his place, except thou repent. 6.
But this thou hast, that thou hatest the deeds of the Nicolaitanes,
which I also hate.7. He that hath an ear, let him hear what the
Spirit saith unto the churches;
To him that overcometh will I give to eat of the tree of life,
which is in the midst of the paradise of God.

For the Church of Ephesus Jesus has good things to say about
them. Jesus is glad that they continue to serve Jesus without giving
up, that they have patience, and that they reject evil. Jesus approved of them because they hated the deeds of the Nicolaitanes,
which Jesus also hated. However Jesus also points out what they
were doing wrong. Jesus says that their love for Him is not as passionate as it once was. They left their first love. Jesus then tells
them what they can do to fix their problem. Jesus tells them to repent and do the first works. The first works would be what they
did for Jesus when they first got saved. Stuff like giving, reading
Scripture, praying, and telling people about Jesus. Finally Jesus
tells them about the reward that they will receive if they do the
things, which He just spoke to them. The reward is that they will
get to eat from the Tree of Life. Remember in the book of Genesis.
God made the Tree of Life.

But God stopped Adam and Eve from eating from the Tree of Life;
otherwise the human race would forever be in their fallen human
sin nature. If Adam and Eve ate from the Tree of Life we would be
eternally separated from God. Which means that we would never
be able to go to Heaven. So God was protecting us from making
the biggest mistake of our life. When we are in Heaven we will
have a new human nature. His Holy Spirit will continuously help
us be righteous people for all of eternity. We will no longer want
to sin. Because of Jesus Christ's redemptive work on the cross,
which cleanses us from all sin; we will be allowed to eat from the
Tree of Life. And this time when we eat from the Tree of Life we
will live forever and we will be in eternal fellowship with God instead of being eternally separated from God.

So to be able to eat from the Tree of Life is an amazing reward for a believer in Jesus Christ. If we keep Jesus as our first love and continuously keep our love for Jesus alive then we shall be able to eat from the Tree of Life. We must always remember how much Jesus loves us. As we think about how much Jesus loves us our love for Jesus will grow. As we think about the goodness, mercy, love, grace, and compassion Jesus has shown us; we will fall absolutely in love with Jesus. Jesus has been so good to me. And I know that Jesus has been good to you too. When I think about the ways that Jesus has shown His mercy to me even when I didn't deserve it; I'm absolutely speechless. I'm in awe of the kindness of Jesus because He has been so good to me. Because of Jesus Christ's love towards me I love Him. Which proves that the verse below is true. Here is the verse.

(1 John 4:19 KJV)

19. We love him, because he first loved us.

Since Jesus loved me first when He died for me on the cross; I love Him. To put it simply I love Jesus because He first loved me.

The Church of Smyrna is called the Persecuted Church. Here is what Jesus had to say to them. Here is the verse.

(Revelation 2:8-11 KJV)

8. And unto the angel of the church in Smyrna write; These things saith the first and the last, which was dead, and is alive; 9. I know thy works, and tribulation, and poverty, (but thou art rich) and I know the blasphemy of them which say they are Jews, and are not, but are the synagogue of Satan. 10. Fear none of those things which thou shalt suffer: behold, the devil shall cast some of you into prison, that ye may be tried; and ye shall have tribulation ten days: be thou faithful unto death, and I will give thee a crown of life. 11. He that hath an ear, let him hear what the Spirit saith unto the churches; He that overcometh shall not be hurt of the second death.

For the Church of Smyrna Jesus was proud that they served Jesus faithfully even though they were going through extreme persecution and they were beyond poor. But Jesus says that even though they are poor on Earth. Jesus says that they are extremely rich in Heaven. This church was storing up treasure in Heaven. This was a faithful church and they kept doing things for Jesus despite persecution; because they were constantly thinking about Heaven and the approval of Jesus. Jesus has nothing bad to say about this church. What Jesus tells them to do is to remain faithful until death. The reward is that they will receive the Crown of Life. If we remain faithful to Jesus until the day we die then one day Jesus will reward us with the Crown of Life. A lifetime of faithful service to Jesus is the wisest thing that we can do. Because one day Jesus will reward us for our faithfulness to Him with the Crown of Life.

The Church of Pergamos is called the Compromising Church. Here is what Jesus had to say to them. Here is the verse.

(Revelation 2:12-17 KJV)

12. And to the angel of the church in Pergamos write; These things saith he which hath the sharp sword with two edges; 13. I know thy works, and where thou dwellest, even where Satan's seat is: and thou holdest fast my name, and hast not denied my faith, even in those days wherein Antipas was my faithful martyr, who was slain among you, where Satan dwelleth. 14. But I have a few things against thee, because thou hast there them that hold the doctrine of Balaam, who taught Balac to cast a stumblingblock before the children of Israel, to eat things sacrificed unto idols, and to commit fornication. 15. So hast thou also them that hold the doctrine of the Nicolaitanes, which thing I hate. 16. Repent; or else I will come unto thee quickly, and will fight against them with the sword of my mouth. 17. He that hath an ear, let him hear what the Spirit saith unto the churches; To him that overcometh will I give to eat of the hidden manna, and will give him a white stone, and in the stone a new name written, which no man knoweth saving he that receiveth it.

For the Church of Pergamos Jesus is extremely happy that they clung tightly to His name because they knew that He was the Author of Life. They did not deny their faith in Jesus even when Antipas was murdered. Jesus hated that the Church of Pergamos tolerated sexual sin, that they tolerated idolatry, and that they even tolerated dangerous heresies from the doctrine of Balaam and the doctrine of the Nicolaitanes.

What Jesus told them to do was to repent. The reward is that they would be able to eat hidden manna and that they would be given a white stone with a new name on it. The cool thing about the white stone is that it says that only the person who receives the white stone can read the new name. So when you try to show someone the stone they will say that they can't read it. It's pretty cool. It's like a hidden message only you and Jesus share with each other. Jesus will give the believer a white stone with their new name on it. I believe the new name on the white stone might be the believer's true character. I believe a person's new name might be based on how that person lived on this Earth before they died. Jesus knows your true character. Take comfort in the fact that while everybody might be saying evil things about you; that Jesus Christ knows your true character deep inside of you.

The movie *The Chronicles of Narnia: The Lion, the Witch and the Wardrobe* does an excellent job with creating a wonderful picture of Jesus giving us a new name of our true character and rewarding us by making us kings and queens of the New Earth. Jesus is the King of kings and the Lord of Lords. Jesus is the Ultimate King and we are the lower kings and queens. In the movie there are four regular kids. Their names are Peter Pevensie, Susan Pevensie, Edmund Pevensie, and Lucy Pevensie. They stumble into a magical land called Narnia; when they go through a magical wardrobe. The King of Narnia is called Aslan. Aslan is the Lion. Aslan represents Jesus Christ.

The character Edmund Pevensie keeps getting into trouble with the White Witch and he keeps telling the White Witch things that are supposed to be kept secret. The White Witch is evil and deceitful. The White Witch represents Satan. Even the White Witch calls Edmund a traitor when Edmund is back with Aslan in Aslan's camp. The White Witch wants to kill Edmund for betraying Aslan. The White Witch says that Edmund must die as payment for his wrong doing. In the same way Satan wants to condemn us to Hell for us sinning against God. Yet Aslan decides to sacrifice Himself to the White Witch in order to save Edmund from being killed. In a similar way Jesus Christ gives His life in order to save us from the penalty of Hell. The White Witch kills Aslan on a stone table with a knife. The White Witch celebrates with her evil minions that the Great Cat is dead. Just like how 2,000 years ago Satan and his demons celebrated after they killed Jesus Christ on the cross thinking that they had defeated Jesus Christ. A day later Aslan comes back to life. Three days later Jesus Christ comes back to life and defeats Death, Sin, Satan, and Hell. Aslan kills the White Witch and peace is restored. One day Jesus Christ will destroy Satan forever and cast Satan into Hell for all eternity. Then Eternal Peace will finally be restored. At the end of the movie all four Pevensie kids become Kings and Queens of Narnia. Even though Aslan knew that Edmund had betrayed him. At the end of the movie Aslan calls Edmund the Just. One day when Jesus rewards us He will not call us by what we did in our sinful lives. But by what we truly are and whose we are. We are Children of God. Jesus will treat us and honor us as Children of God. There is a quote in the Chronicles of Narnia movie that I absolutely love. It gives me excitement and encouragement every time I see it and hear it. I pray this quote encourages you as well.

Here is a quote from Andrew Adamson's film The Chronicles of Narnia: The Lion, the Witch and the Wardrobe.

Aslan: "To the glistening eastern sea, I give you Queen Lucy the Valiant. To the great western woods, King Edmund the Just. To the radiant southern sun, Queen Susan the Gentle. And to the clear northern skies, I give you King Peter the Magnificent. Once a king or queen of Narnia, always a king or queen."

One day Jesus will reward us for our faithfulness to Him in the form of a white stone with a new name on it. Jesus will then make us kings and queens of the New Earth and we will rule over the New Earth forever. It would be cool if Jesus said to us as He places the crowns on our heads. "Once a king or queen of the New Earth, always a king or queen." Jesus will be the Ultimate Ruler but we will get to help rule the New Earth by Jesus Christ's side. Imagine the day when Jesus Christ tells you; your new name. Your new name will be a perfect fit for you and your personality. You will absolutely love the new name that Jesus Christ gives you. Jesus knows the perfect new name for you because He is the One who created you in the first place.

The Church of Thyatira is called the Corrupt Church. Here is what Jesus had to say to them. Here is the verse.

(Revelation 2:18-29 KJV)

18. And unto the angel of the church in Thyatira write; These things saith the Son of God, who hath his eyes like unto a flame of fire, and his feet are like fine brass; 19. I know thy works; and charity, and service, and faith, and thy patience, and thy works; and the last to be more than the first. 20. Notwithstanding I have a few things against thee, because thou sufferest that woman Jezebel, which calleth herself a prophetess, to teach and to seduce my servants to commit fornication, and to eat things sacrificed unto idols. 21. And I gave her space to repent of her fornication; and she repented not. 22. Behold, I will cast her into a bed, and them that commit adultery with her into great tribulation, except they repent of their deeds. 23. And I will kill her children with death; and all the churches shall know that I am he which searcheth the reins and hearts: and I will give unto every one of you according to your works. 24. But unto you I say, and unto the rest in Thyatira as many as have not this doctrine, and which have not known the depths of Satan, as they speak; I will put upon you none other burden. 25. But that which ye have already hold fast till I come. 26. And he that overcometh, and

keepeth my works unto the end, to him will I give power over the nations: 27. And he shall rule them with a rod of iron; as the vessels of a potter shall they be broken to shivers: even as I received of my Father. 28. And I will give him the morning star. 29. He that hath an ear, let him hear what the Spirit saith unto the churches.

To the Church of Thyatira Jesus has good things to say about them. He loves that their love, service, faith, and patience are even greater than before. They have grown in their love like acts of charity. Jesus is angry with the Church of Thyatira because they allowed Jezebel to teach and those who were listening to her are being seduced to commit sexual sin. They also are tolerating idolatry. The thing that Jesus tells them to do is to cling to their faith in Jesus. The reward is that they will be able to rule over the nations and they will also receive the morning star. How cool will it be to rule over nations? You see kings and presidents ruling over nations but those are only temporary. How about ruling over nations forever? When it talks about Jesus giving us the morning star; Jesus is actually saying that He will give us Himself as a reward. Jesus is the reward. Jesus is the morning star. Here is a verse to prove my point.

(Revelation 22:16 KJV)

16. I Jesus have sent mine angel to testify unto you these things in the churches. I am the root and the offspring of David, and the bright and morning star.

Since Jesus is the reward that means that in Heaven we will spend quality time with Jesus. We will share intimate conversations with Jesus. And we will get to learn about Jesus and find out what He truly is like. We will be in fellowship with Jesus everyday for all of eternity. We will have the sweetest friendship with Jesus because we decided to live for Him and not for ourselves.

The Church of Sardis is called the Dead Church. Here is what Jesus said to them. Here is the verse.

(Revelation 3:1-6 KJV)

1. And unto the angel of the church in Sardis write; These things saith he that hath the seven Spirits of God, and the seven stars; I know thy works, that thou livest, and art dead. 2. Be watchful, and strengthen the things which remain, that are ready to die: for I have not found thy works perfect before God. 3. Remember therefore how thou hast received and heard, and hold fast, and repent. If therefore thou shalt not watch, I will come on thee as a thief, and thou shalt not know what hour I will come upon thee. 4. Thou hast a few names even in Sardis which have not defiled their garments; and they shall walk with me in white: for they are worthy. 5. He that overcometh, the same shall be clothed in white raiment; and I will not blot out his name out of the book of life, but I will confess his name before my Father, and before his angels. 6. He that hath an ear, let him hear what the Spirit saith unto the churches.

For the Church of Sardis Jesus was glad that some of them had not defiled their garments and that they had continued to keep their faith in Jesus. The people who did not defile their garments chose not to give into sin. They cared about what Jesus thought of them and lived their lives in righteousness. They believed that the approval of Jesus was far better than the pleasures of sin. Because of their commitment to Jesus to not compromise; they would one day be clothed in beautiful white robes and they would walk with Jesus in Heaven. The thing, which Jesus had against them, is that their works were not perfect before God. Perhaps they were doing good works with the wrong motives.

Jesus told them to repent and to strengthen the things, which remain. The reward is that people who remain faithful to Jesus will one day hear Jesus honor them. They will also be clothed in white garments. Jesus will proudly declare to everyone in Heaven that you are His son or His daughter. Jesus will have a great big smile on His face when he talks about you in front of God the Father and the angels in Heaven.

Jesus won't be ashamed of you. He will be so happy and joyful to express His great love for you. It will be a privilege for Him to give you honor and respect. Even though we don't deserve honor or respect because we are all sinners. Jesus will show His amazing grace and His love to you in the form of praise.

I love it when it talks about us being clothed in white robes. When Jesus gives you the white robe because of your commitment to Him. Because all your life you said no to temptations and you decided that Jesus was more important to you than your sin. When Jesus gives you that white robe it will be a physical thing to show you that Jesus is proud of you. Jesus is showing you in a very tangible way that He is proud of the way you lived your life for Him.

Imagine the day when Jesus gives you the white robe. Let's use our imagination a little bit.

Jesus says to you, "This white robe is for you. Because you were so faithful to Me I want to bless you with the finest robe I can give you. Here put this on."

So you put on the robe. Jesus smiles at you and gives you a big hug.

Jesus says to you, "You look great. Thank you for serving Me even though I know it was difficult for you."

You look at Jesus and say, "Thank you Jesus for blessing me with this amazing robe. I will always want to serve you."

I want to be an overcomer because I want to be clothed in a white robe. I want Jesus to be proud of me. I know that you also want to be clothed in a white robe and have Jesus be proud of you too. Let us all strive to be overcomers. If there is sin in our lives let us get rid of it. Let us keep the approval of Jesus always in our mind. Let us focus on the eternal prize of getting a white robe and hearing Jesus honor us.

The Church of Philadelphia is called the Faithful Church. Here is what Jesus said to them. Here is the verse.

(Revelation 3:7-13 KJV)

7. And to the angel of the church in Philadelphia write; These things saith he that is holy, he that is true, he that hath the key of David, he that openeth, and no man shutteth; and shutteth, and no man openeth; 8. I know thy works: behold, I have set before thee an open door, and no man can shut it: for thou hast a little strength, and hast kept my word, and hast not denied my name. 9. Behold, I will make them of the synagogue of Satan, which say they are Jews, and are not, but do lie; behold, I will make them to come and worship before thy feet, and to know that I have loved thee. 10. Because thou hast kept the word of my patience, I also will keep thee from the hour of temptation, which shall come upon all the world, to try them that dwell upon the earth. 11. Behold, I come quickly: hold that fast which thou hast, that no man take thy crown. 12. Him that overcometh will I make a pillar in the temple of my God, and he shall go no more out: and I will write upon him the name of my God, and the name of the city of my God, which is new Jerusalem, which cometh down out of heaven from my God: and I will write upon him my new name. 13. He that hath an ear, let him hear what the Spirit saith unto the churches.

For the Church of Philadelphia Jesus is overjoyed that they honor Jesus. In other words they give Jesus a good reputation by the way they live their lives for Him. When Christians act like true Christians then people begin to notice that Jesus is real. People who are unbelievers when they see a Christian give their money to someone in need they desire to know what's different about that Christian. They want to know about Jesus because when we live our lives in complete devotion to Jesus then people will want to know how they can be changed also. There is nothing bad that Jesus says about this church. The thing, which Jesus tells them to do, is to keep, trusting in Him. The reward is that they will be a pillar in the temple of God. Which means that they will see Jesus continuously and that they will have an important job to do in His Kingdom. Jesus will also write His new name on them, and the name of the city of God. Jesus will also write the name of God on them. I believe Jesus writes His new name on us because He wants us to know that we are His. We will forever be reminded that we belong to Jesus every time we see His new name written on us. Did you notice that Jesus gets a new name also? I can't wait to find out what Jesus Christ's new name is. I hope you are excited to find out what His new name is also. I believe Jesus writes the name of the city of God on us because it shows us that we are citizens of the Heavenly City.

The Church of Laodicea is called the Lukwarm Church. Here is what Jesus said to them. Here is the verse.

(Revelation 3:14-22 KJV)

14. And unto the angel of the church of the Laodiceans write; These things saith the Amen, the faithful and true witness, the beginning of the creation of God; 15. I know thy works, that thou art neither cold nor hot: I would thou wert cold or hot. 16. So then because thou art lukewarm, and neither cold nor hot, I will spue thee out of my mouth. 17. Because thou sayest, I am rich, and increased with goods, and have need of nothing; and knowest not that thou art wretched, and miserable, and poor, and blind, and naked: 18. I counsel thee to buy of me gold tried in the fire, that thou mayest be rich; and white raiment, that thou mayest be clothed, and that the shame of thy nakedness do not appear; and anoint thine eyes with eye salve, that thou mayest see. 19. As many as I love, I rebuke and chasten: be zealous therefore and repent. 20. Behold, I stand at the door, and knock; if any man hear my voice, and open the door, I will come in to him, and will sup with him, and he with me. 21. To him that overcometh will I grant to sit with me in my throne, even as I also overcame, and am set down with my Father in his throne. 22. He that hath an ear, let him hear what the Spirit saith unto the churches.

For the Church of Laodicea Jesus has nothing good to say about this church. Jesus hated that their works were neutral. They did not have a passion for Jesus as they worked for Him. Jesus told them to repent and be zealous for Him. The reward is that they would share Jesus Christ's throne with Him. When Jesus said that they would sit with Him on His throne he meant that they would have authority. When we overcome we will have a God given position of authority on the New Earth.

We will serve Jesus in His heavenly kingdom. We must always keep our passion for Jesus on fire for Him. If we do that then one day we will get to rule with Jesus on the New Earth.

Now we shall talk about other ways that we can get rewards in Heaven. God will one day reward us just for praying to Him. Here is the verse to prove my point. We can be rewarded by having a consistent prayer life. We have to make prayer a priority in our lives.

(Mathew 6:6 KJV)

6. But thou, when thou prayest, enter into thy closet, and when thou hast shut thy door, pray to thy Father which is in secret; and thy Father which seeth in secret shall reward thee openly.

How amazing will it be to have the Creator of the Universe reward us for the way that we prayed to Him? I believe at that moment we will feel so unworthy and yet at the same time we will agree with Jesus because we know that Jesus doesn't lie. Jesus always tells the truth. Another way of us getting rewards in Heaven is by us doing good things for Jesus. Here is a verse that shows that Jesus will reward us just for doing good works for Him.

(Revelation 22:12 KJV)

12. And, behold, I come quickly; and my reward is with me, to give every man according as his work shall be.

Think about that for a moment. Any good work that we do with the right motive for Jesus will be rewarded one day in Heaven. The Lord Jesus Christ will personally reward us. All of our good deeds that we do for Jesus Christ will one day be rewarded. That old saying that no good deed goes unpunished is the exact opposite of what the Bible actually teaches. The saying should be that all good deeds will be rewarded. I love that Jesus rewards us. I live for that day; when He will reward me. I hope that you are looking forward to that day as well. Here is another verse to show that we should give to people and if we do then we shall be rewarded. Here is the verse.

(Luke 6:38 KJV)

38. Give, and it shall be given unto you; good measure, pressed down, and shaken together, and running over, shall men give into your bosom. For with the same measure that ye mete withal it shall be measured to you again.

Most people think that this verse is talking about giving to get back money. They believe that if they give their money; that God will pay them back with money. But I believe that this verse is talking about us being rewarded in Heaven. Jesus will pay us back in Heaven based on how we generously gave to people in need. When it says that the same measure you use it shall be measured to you again. It is talking about when we give generously to people that Jesus takes notice. Jesus will reward us with as much as He can give us when we are in Heaven with Him.

Here is another way to be rewarded. When we show compassion to our enemies and love them the way Jesus Christ loves them then we will be rewarded. Here is the verse.

(Proverbs 25:21-22 KJV)

21. If thine enemy be hungry, give him bread to eat; and if he be thirsty, give him water to drink: 22. For thou shalt heap coals of fire upon his head, and the LORD shall reward thee.

So why do we get blessed with a reward in Heaven just for showing love towards our enemies? I believe it's because it makes Jesus proud of us when we show compassion to our enemies; because He did the same thing when He was on the cross. Jesus prayed for His enemies even when they nailed Him to the cross. So to show His approval of our lives He blesses us with a reward. When it talks about heaping coals of fire upon his head; I believe it is talking about when we show kindness to our enemies then they start to feel guilty over the way they are treating us. What is really happening is that the Holy Spirit is convicting them of their sin.

Our love towards our enemies is a way that the Holy Spirit chooses to work in an unbeliever's life. Or perhaps it is an enemy that professes to be a Christian but is not really a Christian. Our love towards our enemy will cause them to change their way of living.

As we are generous with our money and give to people who are in desperate need of help. Jesus will reward us. Here are a few Bible verses to prove my point.

(Proverbs 22:9 KJV)

9. He that hath a bountiful eye shall be blessed;
for he giveth of his bread to the poor.

(Matthew 10:42 KJV)

42. And whosoever shall give to drink unto one of these little ones a cup of cold water only in the name of a disciple, verily I say unto you, he shall in no wise lose his reward.

Jesus will not forget your acts of generosity that you have done for Him. He will reward you for all those times you gave to people because you desired to help them. Even when you had a small amount of money and you chose to give to people who needed some food. Jesus is proud of you when you put other people's needs above your own. Here is a verse to prove that we should not only think about our needs but that we should also think about other people's needs as well. Here is the verse.

(Philippians 2:4 KJV)

4. Look not every man on his own things,
but every man also on the things of others.

Jesus cared about our needs not just His own. We needed to be saved from Hell. Jesus put our needs above His own. So much so that He chose to die on a cross for us. Another way to get rewards is to keep your faith in Jesus even when life is terrible and when everything is chaotic in your life. Jesus will reward you because even though you don't see how any good can come out of this terrible situation you still trust Jesus. And that puts a smile on Jesus Christ's face because you still have faith in Him. Here is the verse.

(Hebrews 10:34 KJV)

34. For ye had compassion of me in my bonds, and took joyfully the spoiling of your goods, knowing in yourselves that ye have in heaven a better and an enduring substance.

(2 Corinthians 4:16-18 KJV)

16. For which cause we faint not; but though our outward man perish, yet the inward man is renewed day by day. 17. For our light affliction, which is but for a moment, worketh for us a far more exceeding and eternal weight of glory; 18. While we look not at the things which are seen, but at the things which are not seen are: for the things which are seen are temporal; but the things which are not seen are eternal.

We can have joy even if we lose everything because we know that we have treasure in Heaven. Jesus will make us incredibly wealthy in Heaven. So even if we are poor on Earth one day we will be rich in Heaven. Even when we become old and our body is perishing and getting weaker day by day. Our inward man is flourishing and thriving because we are drawing closer to God day by day. Our hope is in something invisible because the things we can't see are eternal. Something eternal is Heaven. Our painful lives will pale in comparison to the joy that awaits us in Heaven forever. Our sufferings have a purpose. The purpose of our sufferings is that we would learn to become more like Jesus. Plus Jesus will reward us for how we suffered for Him. Jesus is very generous and He will bless the countless Christians who have suffered for His name's sake by rewarding them with rewards beyond they can think or imagine.

Chapter 5

The Book of Life!

It would be wrong for me to tell you about Heaven; but not tell you about the Book of Life. The Book of Life is also sometimes called the Lamb's Book of Life. It is a book in Heaven that has the list of names of the people who are going to Heaven. When a person gets saved their name is written in the Book of Life. We shall now look at some verses in the Bible that talk about the Book of Life. Here are some verses.

(Revelation 20:15 KJV)

15. And whosoever was not found written in the book of life was cast into the lake of fire.

It is very important that your name is written in the Book of Life so that way you won't be cast into the lake of fire. The only way you can get your name in the Book of Life is to believe in Jesus Christ, ask Him to forgive you of your sins, and repent of your sins. Then your name will be written in the Book of Life. Here is another verse about the Book of Life.

(Luke 10:20 KJV)

20. Notwithstanding in this rejoice not, that the spirits are subject unto you; but rather rejoice, because your names are written in heaven.

People sometimes rejoice for the temporary things like their favorite sports team wins, or they get a new job, or they get a new car. When in fact they should be rejoicing for things that are eternal like having their names written in the Book of Life in Heaven.

Here is another verse about the Book of Life.

(Hebrews 12:22-23 KJV)

22. But ye are come unto mount Sion, and unto the city of the living God, the heavenly Jerusalem, and to an innumerable company of angels, 23. To the general assembly and church of the firstborn, which are written in heaven, and to God the Judge of all, and to the spirits of just men made perfect,

One day believers in Jesus Christ who have their names written in the Book of Life will join God, the angels, and they will see the heavenly Jerusalem on the New Earth. Here is another verse about the Book of Life.

(Philippians 4:3 KJV)

3. And I intreat thee also, true yokefellow, help those women which laboured with me in the gospel, with Clement also, and with other my fellowlabourers, whose names are in the book of life.

Those who share the gospel with people are people who want to share the love of Christ with other people. Those people are not in the Book of Life because they share the gospel but only because of their faith in Jesus Christ. As you share your faith in Jesus with other people; know that one day you will meet your Savior Jesus Christ in Heaven. Jesus might even show you the Book of Life and point to your name. How awesome would that be to experience that personally? It will be beyond our wildest dreams and imagination. Here is another verse about the Book of Life.

(Revelation 3:5 KJV)

5. He that overcometh, the same shall be clothed in white
raiment; and I will not blot out his name out of the book of life,
but I will confess his name before my Father,
and before his angels.

The Lord Jesus will never blot out a believer's name from the Book
of Life. This verse is saying that not only will the believer's name
be in the Book of Life but that Jesus will also speak and announce
the believer's name in front of God the Father and in front of His
holy angels. Jesus will honor the believer who overcomes in front
of everyone in Heaven.

Here is another verse about the Book of Life.

(Revelation 21:27 KJV)

27. And there shall in no wise enter into it any thing that defileth,
neither whatsoever worketh abomination, or maketh a lie:
but they which are written in the Lamb's book of life.

You see the only way you will enter Heaven is if you put your faith
in Jesus. Only after you have done that will your name be written
in the Lamb's Book of Life. The reason it is called the Lamb's Book
of Life is because Jesus Christ is called the Lamb of God. Here is
the verse, which speaks about Jesus being called the Lamb of God.

(John 1:29 KJV)

29. The next day John seeth Jesus coming unto him, and saith,
Behold the Lamb of God, which taketh away the sin of the world.

Jesus took away every sin that you have ever committed in the
past, the sins you are committing in the present, and the sins you
will commit in the future. Jesus Christ's blood covers your sins forever. Follow Jesus and thank Him for His mercy on your life. Jesus
loves you with an everlasting love. No matter who you are, what
you have done, wherever you are on the Earth know that Jesus
loves you. Here is another verse about the Book of Life.

(Malachi 3:16-18 KJV)

16. Then they that feared the LORD spake often one to another: and the LORD hearkened, and heard it, and a book of remembrance was written before him for them that feared the LORD, and thought upon his name.

17. And they shall be mine, saith the LORD of hosts, in that day when I make up my jewels; and I will spare them, as a man spareth his own son that serveth him. 18. Then shall ye return, and discern between the righteous and the wicked, between him that serveth God and him that serveth him not.

The Lord Jesus knows those who are serving Him and those who are not serving Him. He even wrote a book to keep track of everyone. He has a special interest in each one of us. Be encouraged my fellow brothers and sisters in Christ. The Lord Jesus is keeping record of how much you serve Him each and everyday.

CHAPTER 6

THE LOVE OF JESUS!

Now we shall talk about the love of Jesus. The only reason we will be allowed into Heaven in the first place is because of Jesus Christ's love for us. Jesus loved us so much that He was willing to leave Heaven and come down to Earth. He was born a baby then he grew up and became a man. He was 30 years old when he began his ministry. For three years he taught people about the kingdom of God and told them how they could be saved through Him. He also healed the sick, raised the dead, rebuked demons. The Pharisees who were the religious leaders in that day wanted to kill Jesus. Jesus had twelve close disciples. One of the disciple's name was Judas. Judas agreed to help the Pharisees. Judas betrayed Jesus for thirty pieces of silver. Jesus was then delivered over to the Pharisees and was later given over to the Romans to be crucified.

It was a horrible death and as Jesus was dying He carried the whole weight of all the sins of the world upon His shoulders. Those sins included the past sins, the present sins, and the future sins of all of humanity. Before Jesus died a thief on the cross who was next to Jesus asked Him to remember him when Jesus came into His kingdom. Jesus said that the thief on the cross would be with Him in Paradise. I love this portion of Scripture because it shows the love of Jesus, the grace of Jesus, the justice of Jesus, and the mercy of Jesus. Here is the verse I hope you are greatly encouraged by it and can see the love of Jesus in this verse.

(Luke 23:42-43 KJV)

42. And he said unto Jesus, Lord, remember me when thou comest into thy kingdom. 43. And Jesus said unto him, Verily I say unto thee, Today shalt thou be with me in paradise.

I love that verse because the thief on the cross was a criminal and yet Jesus loved Him and gave Him assurance where the thief would spend eternity. He would be with Jesus in Heaven forever. The thief did not do any good works before he died which just shows you that doing good works can't get you to Heaven. The thief did not have to do any good works because all He did was put His faith in Jesus. Even though good works can't save us; we do good works because it is out of our joy of being saved that we want to do good works for Jesus. Plus we were created to do good works. God wants us to do good works. Here is the verse that talks about that specifically.

(Ephesians 2:10 KJV)

10. For we are his workmanship, created in Christ Jesus unto good works, which God hath before ordained that we should walk in them.

Now you may be wondering but how do I do good works? I don't have the capability to do that. You would be right in thinking that. Thankfully the Bible gives us the answer to that problem. In fact God is the answer. Here is the verse.

(Philippians 2:13 KJV)

13. For it is God which worketh in you both to will and to do of his good pleasure.

It is God who will help you to do the good works. Just ask God for His help. Talk to Him and then do the good work for Him. I have not even told you the best part. Three days later after Jesus died on the cross He rose from the dead. He then stayed on the Earth for 40 more days and then He ascended up into Heaven. Jesus now sits at the right hand of God in Heaven. Now I would like to share with you some verses about Jesus Christ's love. To show you that Jesus loves people, He loves me, and He loves you. Here are the verses.

(John 11:5 KJV)

5. Now Jesus loved Martha, and her sister, and Lazarus.

(John 13:23 KJV)

23. Now there was leaning on Jesus' bosom one of his disciples, whom Jesus loved.

(John 15:9-10 KJV)

9. As the Father hath loved me, so have I loved you: continue ye in my love. 10. If ye keep my commandments, ye shall abide in my love; even as I have kept my Father's commandments, and abide in his love.

(Galatians 2:20 KJV)

20. I am crucified with Christ: nevertheless I live; yet not I, but Christ liveth in me: and the life which I now live in the flesh I live by the faith of the Son of God, who loved me, and gave himself for me.

(Jeremiah 31:3 KJV)

3. The LORD hath appeared of old unto me, saying, Yea, I have loved thee with an everlasting love: therefore with lovingkindness have I drawn thee.

(Romans 5:8 KJV)

8. But God commendeth his love toward us, in that while we were yet sinners, Christ died for us.

I will give you one example of how Jesus showed His love to someone who was in need. A person who desperately needed to be comforted. It is an extraordinary example. Here is the verse.

(Luke 7:12-15 KJV)

12. Now when he came nigh to the gate of the city, behold, there was a dead man carried out, the only son of his mother, and she was a widow: and much people of the city was with her. 13. And when the Lord saw her, he had compassion on her, and said unto her, Weep not. 14. And he came and touched the bier: and they that bare him stood still. And he said, Young man, I say unto thee, Arise. 15. And he that was dead sat up, and began to speak. And he delivered him to his mother.

Jesus saw the broken heart of the widow who was also a mother. He saw that she was devastated over the death of her son. So Jesus raised her son back from the dead. Imagine the joy on that mother's face when she saw her son alive again. That was definitely an extraordinary day for the both of them. It was a glorious day for the mother as well as the son as they were reunited. I bet Jesus was smiling after He raised the son from the dead because He saw the joy on that mother's face. That is the kind of God we serve. We serve a God who not only has absolute power over death but we also serve a God who has a compassionate heart.

I hope you can see the love of Jesus in those verses. Focus on how much Jesus loves you. It is a very comforting thing to think about. There is a verse that has always comforted me. For some reason I just love this specific verse. It is probably because Jesus will accept anyone who comes to Him. Here is the verse.

(John 6:37 KJV)

37. All that the Father giveth me shall come to me; and him that
cometh to me I will in no wise cast out.

Jesus will never reject anyone who comes to Him. He will forgive anyone who is willing to ask Him for His forgiveness of their sins. He will love them, protect them, guide them, and finally He will take them to be with Him in Heaven forever.

Now we shall talk about the moment you die and what you will experience after you die. Here is a verse explaining what happens when you die.

(Luke 16:19-23 KJV)

19. There was a certain rich man, which was clothed in purple
and fine linen, and fared sumptuously every day: 20. And there
was a certain beggar named Lazarus, which was laid at his gate,
full of sores, 21. And desiring to be fed with the crumbs which
fell from the rich man's table: moreover the dogs came and
licked his sores. 22. And it came to pass that the beggar died, and
was carried by the angels into Abraham's bosom: the rich man
also died, and was buried; 23. And in hell he lift up his eyes,
being in torments, and seeth Abraham afar off,
and Lazarus in his bosom.

The rich man went to Hell after he died. He did not go to Hell because he was rich. He went to Hell because he had no place in his heart for God. For the unbeliever when they die they go to Hell and they are immediately in torment forever. They will experience a terrible darkness and piercing hot flames of fire.

The beggar Lazarus went to Heaven after he died. For the believer in Christ when they die; angels carry them to Heaven. How wonderful is Jesus Christ's love for us that He would send us angels to take us to Heaven? It is beyond our capacity to comprehend Jesus Christ's love for us. Jesus loves us so much that He will not allow us to be alone at the moment of our death. At the exact moment we die He will send His angels to comfort us and to usher us into the presence of Jesus Christ in Heaven.

I have another Bible verse that explains what a believer in Jesus Christ experiences when they die. Here is the verse.

(2 Corinthians 5:8 KJV)

8. We are confident, I say, and willing rather to be absent from the body, and to be present with the Lord.

To be absent from the body means to die. To be present with the Lord means you will be with Jesus Christ in Heaven. As soon as you die you will immediately be in Heaven and you will see Jesus Christ face to face.

Now we shall talk about our love for Jesus Christ and His love for us.

(John 14:15 KJV)

15. If ye love me, keep my commandments.

(John 14:21 and 23 KJV)

21. He that hath my commandments, and keepeth them, he it is that loveth me: and he that loveth me shall be loved of my Father, and I will love him, and will manifest myself to him.

23. Jesus answered and said unto him, If a man love me, he will keep my words: and my Father will love him, and we will come unto him, and make our abode with him.

(John 13:34-35 KJV)

34. A new commandment I give unto you, That ye love one another; as I have loved you, that ye also love one another. 35. By this shall all men know that ye are my disciples, if ye have love one to another.

I have a Bible verse that I absolutely love because it talks about how Jesus Christ wants a relationship with us. This Bible verse is Jesus Christ speaking to us. Here is the verse.

(Revelation 3:20 KJV)

20. Behold, I stand at the door, and knock: if any man hear my voice, and open the door, I will come in to him, and will sup with him, and he with me.

Jesus Christ is a relational God. Jesus Christ wants to have a relationship with each one of us because He loves us. Jesus wants to spend time with us, talk with us, laugh with us, and even eat with us in Heaven and also in the future on the New Earth. How cool will it be to share a meal with Jesus who is also the One who created you? Now there is something amazing and so simple that you might have noticed in the verses above that talked about how we truly show our love for Jesus. The way we show that we love Jesus is that we obey His commandments. Another way of saying it is that we follow or keep His commandments.

And what are the commandments that we should keep to show our love for Jesus? There are only two commandments that we keep to show our love for Jesus Christ. The first commandment is to love God. The second commandment is to love people. Here is the verse to show the two commandments that we follow to show our love for Jesus. This Bible verse is Jesus Christ speaking.

(Mark 12:30-31 KJV)

30. And thou shalt love the Lord thy God with all thy heart, and with all thy soul, and with all thy mind, and with all thy strength: this is the first commandment. 31. And the second is like, namely this, Thou shalt love thy neighbour as thyself. There is none other commandment greater than these.

The great part is as we follow Jesus Christ's commandments to love God and love people. Jesus says that He will love us and also that God the Father will love us as well. I would like to talk about what we as Christians have to go through each and every day. Whenever we sin we feel condemned. Our thoughts are telling us each and every day that we are worthless or that we are not saved because a child of God would never do what we just did. But those lies and condemnation are from the enemy who is called Satan, the Devil, the Accuser of our brethren, or Lucifer.

I would like to show you a Bible verse that explains what Satan does every day and night to hurt us and make us discouraged. Satan wants to make us feel condemned. Here is the verse.

(Revelation 12:9-11 KJV)

9. And the great dragon was cast out, that old serpent called the Devil, and Satan, which deceiveth the whole world: he was cast out into the earth, and his angels were cast out with him. 10. And I heard a loud voice saying in heaven, Now is come salvation, and strength, and the kingdom of our God, and the power of his Christ: for the accuser of our brethren is cast down, which accused them before our God day and night. 11. And they overcame him by the blood of the Lamb, and by the word of their testimony; and they loved not their lives unto the death.

Satan is called the accuser of our brethren. Every single day and night Satan tells God what each of us did that day. Satan wants God to judge us because of the sins that we commit every single day. Satan wants to destroy us.

Every day Satan is condemning us in front of God. Every time we sin; Satan is right there whispering his condemnation and lies in our thoughts. But the love of Jesus Christ is amazing. The grace of our Lord Jesus Christ is beyond comprehension.

(John 1:12 KJV)

12. But as many as received him, to them gave he power to become the sons of God, even to them that believe on his name:

Those who receive Jesus Christ as their Lord and Savior become sons and daughters of God.

(2 Corinthians 5:17 KJV)

17. Therefore if any man be in Christ, he is a new creature: old things are passed away; behold, all things are become new.

Once you are a child of God you become a new creature. Or to put it simply you become a new person. Your lifestyle changes because you begin to have a new heart that has been transformed by God Himself. Your attitudes, thoughts, and feelings towards people change. Here is a verse that explains my point about God putting a new heart in you. Here is the verse.

(Ezekiel 11:19 KJV)

19. And I will give them one heart, and I will put a new spirit within you; and I will take the stony heart out of their flesh, and will give them an heart of flesh:

When you get a new heart you become more sensitive to the things of God. You will want to do the things that honor God. You will look at sin in a different way. Before you came to Jesus Christ you sinned like crazy. But now that you have a new heart you struggle with your sin. You don't want to sin because you know it would make God sad. You have this desire to keep yourself pure so that you honor Jesus Christ. You have this struggle inside you because of your new heart. God gives you a new heart when you accept Jesus Christ as your Lord and Savior. You have this tug of war in your heart. On the one side you want to sin but on the other side you want to stop sinning because of your love for Jesus.

The apostle Paul explains this tug of war with sin and loyalty to Jesus Christ.

Here is the verse.

(Romans 7:19-25 KJV)

19. For the good that I would I do not: but the evil which I would not, that I do. 20. Now if I do that I would not, it is no more I that do it, but sin that dwelleth in me. 21. I find then a law, that, when I would do good, evil is present with me. 22. For I delight in the law of God after the inward man: 23. But I see another law in my members, warring against the law of my mind, and bringing me into captivity to the law of sin which is in my members. 24. O wretched man that I am! who shall deliver me from the body of this death? 25. I thank God through Jesus Christ our Lord. So then with the mind I myself serve the law of God; but with the flesh the law of sin.

Jesus Christ is the only person who can help us overcome our sinful nature. We need to depend on Jesus Christ daily. We need to ask for His help each time a temptation comes our way. We need His help in order to resist temptation. There is a verse that tells us how after we have become a new person in Christ; what we should do with our old sinful lifestyle. Here is the verse.

(Ephesians 4:22-24 KJV)

22. That ye put off concerning the former conversation the old man, which is corrupt according to the deceitful lusts; 23. And be renewed in the spirit of your mind; 24. And that ye put on the new man, which after God is created in righteousness and true holiness.

When it says put off concerning the former conversation that is just talking about how you should stop doing the old ways in which you lived your life before you came to Jesus Christ. The old man refers to our sinful nature or more specifically our sinful lifestyle. The new man refers to our new nature in Jesus Christ. We are to stop our former way of living in sin. And we are to start living righteously in

Jesus Christ. In short you can break this verse down into two things. Stop doing bad things and start doing good things.

When it says be renewed in the spirit of your mind. That is talking about filling our minds with God's Truth. The only way we get God's Truth is if we read the Bible.

(Romans 8:1 KJV)

1. There is therefore now no condemnation to them which are in Christ Jesus, who walk not after the flesh, but after the Spirit.

You are no longer condemned to Hell if you believe in Jesus Christ because you then become a child of God.

(1 John 2:1-2 KJV)

1. My little children, these things write I unto you, that ye sin not. And if any man sin, we have an advocate with the Father, Jesus Christ the righteous: 2. And he is the propitiation for our sins: and not for ours only, but also for the sins of the whole world.

So picture this verse as a Heavenly Court scene. Let's use our imagination. God the Father is the Judge. Jesus Christ is the Lawyer for us. Satan is the Prosecutor against us. And you and me are the defendants in the Heavenly Court Room scared to death about the outcome. We have been charged with many sinful crimes against the Heavenly Father God. Satan is accusing us trying to get God the Father the Judge to condemn us to Hell. Meanwhile God the Father the Judge is listening to Satan's accusations and charges against us. After Satan is finished with his accusations and charges against us. Jesus Christ our lawyer gets up from the chair and tells God the Father the Judge that our sinful crimes have been paid for by Jesus Christ's own blood.

God the Father the Judge says in the Heavenly Court Room. "The crimes have been paid for and these charges against these defendants have been dismissed."

Every single one of us in that Heavenly Court Room has a sigh of relief. We are amazed at the grace of God. Let's make it even more personal.

Jesus Christ might even say to God the Father the Judge, "Hey Dad I know that Satan has brought these accusations and charges against Nick; but remember I already paid for Nick's sins and crimes. Remember I went to the cross and died for his sins with my blood. My Blood washes away his sins. There is no need to condemn Nick to Hell because I have already paid the price for his freedom. I love Nick with an everlasting love."

Whatever your name is. Just replace my name with your name. Jesus is saying those words about you everyday. He loves you and wants you to be with Him in Heaven.

CHAPTER 7

A GREAT REUNION IN HEAVEN AND THE RAPTURE!

Imagine one day of seeing your loved ones who have already died in Christ. You don't have to imagine because one day you will see them in Heaven. Whether you die and go home to be with the Lord or if you are raptured with the Church while you are still alive. Either way you will be reunited with your dear family members and friends in Christ. The Rapture of the Church is the hope of the Church. As Christians we have the hope of seeing Jesus and being reunited with our loved ones who have died and have put their faith in Jesus Christ. This hope is what we Christians call the Rapture. The Rapture gives the Church hope because we know that any day, any month, or any year we will be reunited with our loved ones and we will be with Jesus in Heaven forever. We will meet Jesus in the clouds and be eternally happy. I would like to show you some Bible verses that talk about the Rapture. Here are the verses.

(1Corinthians 15:51-53 KJV)

51. Behold, I shew you a mystery; We shall not all sleep, but we shall all be changed, 52. In a moment, in the twinkling of an eye, at the last trump: for the trumpet shall sound, and the dead shall be raised incorruptible, and we shall be changed.
53. For this corruptible must put on incorruption, and this mortal must put on immortality.

When it says in a moment, in the twinkling of an eye that means that the Rapture will happen instantly. The Rapture could happen at any moment. Here is another verse about the Rapture and it specifically talks about how we should live our lives before Jesus Christ returns for us, which is the Rapture of the Church.

(1John 2:28 KJV)

28. And now, little children, abide in him; that, when he shall appear, we may have confidence,
and not be ashamed before him at his coming.

When it says abide in Him it is talking about abiding in Jesus Christ. By repenting of our sins and choosing to live righteously for Jesus Christ we are abiding in Him. The Rapture could happen at any moment, which is why we need to be ready for it by the way we live our lives. Jesus Christ could return at any moment. I don't want to be caught in sin when the Rapture happens and then I see Jesus face to face. That would devastate me completely. I would be ashamed to see Jesus because I know that I let Him down. Let not that happen to any of us. We should live in such a way that we won't be ashamed to see Jesus. In fact we will be joy filled to see Jesus because we know that we did our best to please Him by how we lived for Him. Here is another verse about the Rapture that Jesus Christ Himself spoke.

(John 14:2-3 KJV)

2. In my Father's house are many mansions: if it were not so, I would have told you. I go to prepare a place for you. 3. And if I go and prepare a place for you, I will come again, and receive you unto myself; that where I am, there ye may be also.

Jesus is working on a special mansion for each believer in Jesus Christ every single day. One day each believer in Jesus Christ will live in their own specific heavenly mansion when they are in Heaven. The place He is preparing for us is Heaven. Jesus is using

His infinite creativity to wow us and blow our minds when it comes to Heaven. He wants us to be in awe of Heaven continuously for all of eternity. Which is why He has been working on Heaven for so long. The way Jesus will bring us to Heaven if we are still alive on planet Earth is the Rapture of the Church.

The best part for those people who are still alive on planet Earth when the Rapture of the Church happens is that those people will never have to experience death. I believe that Jesus is building each mansion in Heaven with each specific person in mind. Jesus will make each mansion in Heaven customized for that person. Whatever that person loves will be in their mansion. Jesus is a personal God so why wouldn't we expect Him to build a mansion in Heaven that matches that person's personality.

I hope my mansion is filled with beautiful music. I love listening to music. Here is a verse that actually describes the Rapture in great detail. Almost like a step-by-step process.

(1Thessalonians 4:13-18 KJV)

13. But I would not have you to be ignorant, brethren, concerning them which are asleep, that ye sorrow not, even as others which have no hope. 14. For if we believe that Jesus died and rose again, even so them also which sleep in Jesus will God bring with him. 15. For this we say unto you by the word of the Lord, that we which are alive and remain unto the coming of the Lord shall not prevent them which are asleep. 16. For the Lord himself shall descend from heaven with a shout, with the voice of the archangel, and with the trump of God: and the dead in Christ shall rise first: 17. Then we which are alive and remain shall be caught up together with them in the clouds, to meet the Lord in the air: and so shall we ever be with the Lord.
18.Wherefore comfort one another with these words.

When it says those who sleep in Jesus that just means any believer of Jesus Christ who has died. The dead in Christ will rise from the dead then the believers in Jesus Christ who are still alive on planet

Earth will be caught up in the clouds where we will see the Lord. We will also see our family, friends, the saints of the New Testament, the saints of the Old Testament of the Bible, and every believer in Jesus Christ who has ever lived and died. Imagine if at the Rapture of the Church when you are looking at the Lord Jesus Christ in the clouds that standing (or floating) right beside you is Moses, Elijah, David, Gideon, the apostle Peter, the apostle Paul, your brothers, your sisters, your grandparents, your Mom, your Dad, or even your best friend.

Imagine a daughter who had to say goodbye to her father due to death. Now imagine the joy on that daughter's face when she sees her father again in Heaven. That will be extraordinary. Or a son who had to say a tearful goodbye to his mother whom he loved very much. That son will be beyond happy when he sees his mother again in Heaven. That is why the apostle Paul told us to comfort one another with these words; as we keep our focus on the Rapture of the Church. Imagine living forever and never having to say goodbye to your dearly loved one. You will never be interrupted again in your relationship with the person you love; with the bitter taste of death.

There will be joy, happiness, love, security, intimacy, companionship, and perfect relationships in Heaven forever. How great and exciting will that reunion be? I can't wait to experience that personally. That is my hope. My hope is one day that I will see my Savior Jesus Christ face to face.

Now we shall talk about what we will experience at the Rapture. This verse talks about what Jesus Christ will experience and what we will experience at the Rapture. Here is the verse.

(2 Thessalonians 1:10 KJV)

10. When he shall come to be glorified in his saints, and to be admired in all them that believe (because our testimony among you was believed) in that day.

When Jesus comes back for His Church and we meet Jesus in the air we will look at Jesus Christ with pure awe and wonder. We will want to just look at Jesus and give Him the praise He truly deserves. We will admire Him and thank Him for all He has done for us. We will want to spend the rest of eternity just learning about Jesus. We will have our eternal relationship with Jesus strengthened and come alive before our very eyes by actually having conversations with Him, eating meals with Him, playing with Him, and laughing with Him. Jesus will finally get the praise from men that He deserves.

CHAPTER 8

JOYOUS SINGING IN HEAVEN!

Out of all the things that we do here on Earth; there is one thing that we can do on Earth; that we will also be able to do in Heaven. That one thing is singing and worshipping God. My sister Stephanie is on the worship team at the church that I attend. She loves to sing to God and she plays on her guitar for hours and she never gets tired of doing that. She finds pure pleasure in worshipping her Savior Jesus Christ. God has given her an amazing singing voice and it is a joy to hear her sing. I know that my sister will love to sing in Heaven when it is time to sing.

For those of you who don't like to sing don't worry about it. I promise you it won't be an unending worship service in Heaven. But when we do sing in Heaven it will be enjoyable, it will not be a burden to sing, it will be exciting, passionate, enthusiastic, and the best part about singing in Heaven and worshipping Jesus Christ is that we will see Him face to face. We will see Jesus as we sing to Him, which will just cause us to sing more passionate and joyful to Him. We will be happy as we worship Jesus. Now I would like to show you some verses that describe the joy of singing to God. The first verse I will show you is found in the book of Revelation. This verse talks about people in Heaven singing to God. Here is the verse.

(Revelation 5:9-10 KJV)

9. And they sung a new song, saying, Thou art worthy to take the book, and to open the seals thereof: for thou wast slain, and hast redeemed us to God by thy blood out of every kindred, and

tongue, and people, and nation; 10. And hast made us unto our God kings and priests: and we shall reign on the earth.

I love this song that they sing in Heaven because it focuses on what Jesus did for us at the cross to pay for our sins with His blood and to bring us back to God. But it does not stop there; it then says what we will experience in the future. It says that we are kings and priests for God and that we shall reign on the Earth. When it says that we shall reign on the Earth it is talking about the New Earth. It is good to sing to God. Godly people should get their joy from singing to God. Don't take my word for it let's see what the Bible has to say about singing to God. Here are some verses that talk about the joy of singing to God.

(Psalm 33:1-3 KJV)

1. Rejoice in the LORD, O ye righteous: for praise is comely for the upright. 2. Praise the LORD with harp: sing unto him with the psaltery and an instrument of ten strings. 3. Sing unto him a new song; play skillfully with a loud noise.

Praising God is a good thing that upright people should do. Here is another verse.

(Psalm 5:11 KJV)

11. But let all those that put their trust in thee rejoice: let them ever shout for joy, because thou defendest them: let them also that love thy name be joyful in thee.

As we put our trust in Jesus we can have joy and happiness because we know that Jesus will defend us. Here is another verse.

(Psalm 96:1-2 KJV)

1. O sing unto the Lord a new song: sing unto the Lord, all the earth. 2. Sing unto the Lord, bless his name; shew forth his salvation from day to day.

The word shew is just another way of saying show. So when it says shew forth his salvation from day to day that just means that we need to show people each day how Jesus can save them and how Jesus has saved us. We need to tell people each day that Jesus Christ can save anyone who comes to Him by faith and believes in Him. Whoever repents of their sins, believes in Jesus Christ, receives Jesus Christ into their heart, and asks Him for His forgiveness of their sins will be saved. We can share our testimony to people as a way to bring glory to God. I bet Jesus smiles every time He sees us share our testimony with someone; as we tell them what Jesus has done in our lives.

Be encouraged and never be afraid to tell your story to someone who may desperately need to hear what Jesus has done in your life.

If they see and hear what Jesus has done for you then believe me they will want Jesus to do the same thing for them as well. Here is another verse.

(Psalm 13:6 KJV)

6. I will sing unto the LORD,
because he hath dealt bountifully with me.

Bountifully means giving generously. We should sing to Jesus because He has given us so much. He gave us His life on the cross, which allowed us to go to Heaven when we die. Just think about how much God blesses you each and every day and then praise Him for His generosity. Then be generous with other people. As Christians we are to be generous and we are supposed to be a light to people with our good works. Here are two verses that talk about being generous and our good works to people. Let these verses encourage you.

(Proverbs 11:24-25 KJV)

24. There is that scattereth, and yet increaseth; and there is that withholdeth more than is meet, but it tendeth to poverty. 25. The liberal soul shall be made fat: and he that watereth shall be watered also himself.

The person who keeps their money and never gives their money away to people in need will be miserable and it will lead to their own poverty. It will feel like they are always short on cash. Even though they keep their money close to their chests they will one day have no money because all they cared about was themselves. The stock market could crash, or they could lose their job, or an unexpected illness could come upon them and then they would be covered in great amounts of hospitals bills. However the liberal soul means someone who is generous with money. The person who keeps giving money away will not be left without any money. In fact they will have enough money to keep doing life.

Another way of saying it is that the generous person who gives money away to someone who is in need; that same generous person will also be provided for.

God will take care of the generous person to make sure their financial needs are met. It is right there in the text when it says he that watereth shall be watered also himself. As you give your money away to people in need you will have enough money to support yourself. I'm not saying generous people will be blessed with incredible wealth. There are some who are blessed in that way and there are others who are not. What I'm saying is that the generous person will have their financial needs met. Whatever that amount is or in whatever way that God decides to provide for that person financially that is up to God to decide. Here is the verse that talks about good works and why we should do them so that people will see them and give glory to God.

(Matthew 5:16 KJV)

16. Let your light so shine before men, that they may see your good works, and glorify your Father which is in heaven.

So as we are doing good works for people and showing the light of Jesus in our lives with them; then these people will have no other choice but to give glory to God. There will be no other explanation that these people can come up with to explain why we do good things for other people and why we live so radically for Jesus except for one reason, and that is that Jesus Christ is real. This verse talks about how God will sing for us because He wants to and because He delights to express His love for us in that way. Here is the verse.

(Zephaniah 3:17 KJV)

17. The Lord thy God in the midst of thee is mighty; he will save, he will rejoice over thee with joy; he will rest in his love, he will joy over thee with singing.

God gives us rest because of His love for us. We can rest in God's love for us. God will one day sing for us to express His great love for us. God is the One who invented singing in the first place. I bet God has the most amazing singing voice ever. God's singing voice will be unlike anything or anyone we have ever heard sing before. I believe that in Heaven God will give each of us perfect singing voices. Which is good for me because I can't sing at all. My singing voice stinks.

My sister tells me that I should not be on the worship team at our church and I agree with her completely. In short singing in Heaven will be amazing, joyous, wonderful, and beyond anything we have imagined or have even experienced on this Earth. There might even be new musical instruments in Heaven that we have never seen before. I believe there will be new songs in Heaven because God loves new songs and because He wants us to use our creative ability to worship Him in new ways particularly new songs. We shall look at two final verses about why we should sing to God.

(Psalm 147:1- 4 KJV)

1. Praise ye the Lord: for it is good to sing praises unto our God; for it is pleasant; and praise is comely. 2. The Lord doth build up Jerusalem: he gathereth together the outcasts of Israel. 3. He healeth the broken in heart, and bindeth up their wounds.
4. He telleth the number of the stars;
he calleth them all by their names.

We should praise God because it is good for us. We should praise God because He cares about us. But we should praise God because God is the only One who can fix us and heal our broken hearts. Plus God is our Creator. He created all the stars in the sky and He knows each star by name.

(Ephesians 5:19-20 KJV)

19. Speaking to yourselves in psalms and hymns and spiritual songs, singing and making melody in your heart to the Lord; 20. Giving thanks always for all things unto God and the Father in the name of our Lord Jesus Christ;

Finally we should give praise to God because it is our way of thanking Him for all He has done for us.

CHAPTER 9

THE JUDGMENT SEAT OF CHRIST!

When you think about the Judgment Seat of Christ what comes to your mind? Fear? Excitement? Regret? Happiness? Guilt? Joy? Shame? Honored? If you are a Christian who is living in sin and have not repented of your sins then I would expect that you might feel fear, regret, guilt, and shame when you see Jesus at the Judgment Seat of Christ. But if you have repented of your sins and are doing good works for Jesus then I would expect you to feel excitement, happiness, joy, and honored when you see Jesus at the Judgment Seat of Christ. The Judgment Seat of Christ is also called the Bema. The Greek word for Judgment Seat is the Bema. In ancient times when the people would play the Isthmian Games there was a raised platform where a judge would sit to judge and give out awards to winners of the games. That is what the Judgment Seat of Christ or the Bema is all about. Jesus will judge your life and then He will reward you.

The Judgment Seat of Christ is a judgment in which Jesus Christ will decide how much authority and rewards He will bless us with. The Judgment Seat of Christ will determine our position in Jesus Christ's Kingdom on the New Earth. I want to make something perfectly clear. The Judgment Seat of Christ does not determine whether we are saved or not. The Judgment Seat of Christ determines how much authority and rewards are given to us for all of eternity. The rewards are based on the way that we lived for Jesus while we were still alive on the Earth before we died. In other words, the way that we live for Jesus today on Earth determines what our future experience, heavenly rewards, and authority will be like on the New Earth. To put it simply. Our present way of living on Earth today determines our future way of living on the New Earth. The way we live today will determine how we will live in eternity. Our position of authority on the New Earth will be determined by how we live for Jesus today on the Earth.

(Mark 9:41 KJV)

41. For whosoever shall give you a cup of water to drink in my name, because ye belong to Christ, verily I say unto you, he shall not lose his reward.

Every act of generosity that we do for people will be rewarded at the Judgment Seat of Christ.

(Matthew 20:16 KJV)

16. So the last shall be first, and the first last: for many be called, but few chosen.

In God's economy the roles will be reversed. People who have served tirelessly for the Lord Jesus Christ will be honored. People who were never thought of as important on Earth will one day be famous and honored in Heaven. The faithful servants of Jesus Christ will be the first in Heaven. People who did not want to serve Jesus on the Earth but only wanted to be served by others will be the last in Heaven. A person who is serving the Lord Jesus Christ their entire life will be rewarded at the Judgment Seat of Christ. The fact that we get rewarded for our good deeds that we did for Jesus is just another way of God showing His Grace towards us. We don't deserve anything. What we deserve is Hell. Yet in God's grace He will graciously lavish us with eternal heavenly rewards.

The Judgment Seat of Christ is when believers in Christ will have to give an account of their lives to Jesus about how they lived for Him. The Judgment Seat of Christ is also when Jesus will reward believers in Christ with eternal rewards for their faithful service to Him. The Judgment Seat of Christ is not what determines the believer's salvation. Their salvation was already paid for and secured when Jesus died on the cross for them. The Judgment Seat of Christ will be like an award ceremony for believers who have faithfully served Jesus. Now I would like to show you some verses that talk about the Judgment Seat of Christ.

(Romans 14:10-12 KJV)

10. But why dost thou judge thy brother? or why dost thou set at nought thy brother? for we shall all stand before the judgment seat of Christ. 11. For it is written, As I live, saith the Lord, every knee shall bow to me, and every tongue shall confess to God. 12. So then every one of us shall give account of himself to God.

We will individually have to stand alone in front of Jesus Christ and explain to Him the reason we chose to live our lives the way that we did on the Earth. The Judgment Seat of Christ will be public but it will also be personal. Each of us will have our own intimate conversations with Jesus. Here is another verse that talks about the Judgment Seat of Christ.

(2 Corinthians 5:10 KJV)

10. For we must all appear before the judgment seat of Christ; that every one may receive the things done in his body, according to that he hath done, whether it be good or bad.

When it speaks about the things done in the body whether good or bad it is talking about two different things. When it talks about the good things done in the body it is talking about us being rewarded for the good things we have done for Jesus Christ because our motives were godly. Our motives or desires was to bring glory to God. When it talks about the bad things done in the body it is talking about us losing a reward because our motives were wrong. Our motives were selfish and all about us. Here is another verse about the Judgment Seat of Christ.

(1 Corinthians 3:10-15 KJV)

10. According to the grace of God which is given unto me, as a wise masterbuilder, I have laid the foundation, and another buildeth thereon. But let every man take heed how he buildeth thereupon. 11. For other foundation can no man lay that is laid, which is Jesus Christ. 12. Now if any man build upon this foundation gold, silver, precious stones, wood, hay, stubble; 13. Every man's work shall be made manifest: for the day shall declare it, because it shall be revealed by fire; and the fire shall try every man's work of what sort it is. 14. If any man's work abide which he hath built thereupon, he shall receive a reward. 15. If any man's work shall be burned, he shall suffer loss: but he himself shall be saved; yet so as by fire.

At the Judgment Seat of Christ our works, which we have done for Jesus will be judged. Jesus Christ will be the Judge. Precious stones are the good motives of our heart, that we did good works to bring glory to Jesus. Wood is the bad motives of our heart, that we did good works to bring glory to ourselves. Precious stones are good works that we have done that have eternal significance. Wood is the things that we have done that don't have any eternal significance.

I would like to give you two examples of the building materials and motives of the heart.

Let's say you tell someone about the gospel because you want them to get saved. That would be considered precious stones and that would have eternal significance. You would get an award in Heaven because your good work passed through the fire.

Now let's say you give money to someone so you that you can be admired by other people. That is called pride. The motive was all about you getting the praise. That would be considered wood. That wouldn't have any eternal significance. You wouldn't have an award because it would be burned up in the fire.

On the day that we stand at the Judgment Seat of Christ our works, which we have done for Jesus will be tested by fire. Our rewards in Heaven will be determined by how we were faithful to Jesus in this life, how we resisted temptation, how we shared the gospel with people, how we gave to people in need, and how we prayed continuously for people who needed prayer. I know there are many people who say that our good works don't matter to God; because our good works can't save us. But they forget that God will reward us for our good works. If you think that being faithful to God amounts to nothing; and that there is no purpose in being diligent towards Him then think again. Here is a verse that talks about God rewarding us for our diligence towards Him. Here is the verse.

(Hebrews 11:6 KJV)

6. But without faith it is impossible to please him: for he that cometh to God must believe that he is, and that he is a rewarder of them that diligently seek him.

Diligently seeking God is reading the Bible, praying, giving, and sharing the gospel with people. Also Jesus said that He has rewards, which He will bring with Him to give to His people who are faithful to Him. Here is the verse.

(Revelation 22:12 KJV)

12. And, behold, I come quickly; and my reward is with me, to give every man according as his work shall be.

Since Jesus will reward each person for the good works that they have done. Then I want to do as many good works as I possibly can. I hope you want to do the same. Just remember every good work that you do for Jesus Christ will be rewarded. To put it another way if we are going to live in Heaven forever don't you want to have some stuff in your mansion? You don't want to be broke in Heaven. Imagine if you see other people getting rewards at the Judgment Seat of Christ but you have no rewards at all. How depressed would you feel? That is why it is important to do good works for Jesus before you die that way you will have rewards in Heaven at the Judgment Seat of Christ.

Do yourself a favor for your eternal future in Heaven and do good works for Jesus. Give money to people in need, pray for people who need salvation, share the gospel to people, resist temptation, and choose not to sin. You will be eternally grateful that you did those things because at the Judgment Seat of Christ you will have many rewards. I would now like to show you a parable that Jesus Himself spoke about rewards in Heaven for faithful service to Jesus. Here is the parable.

(Matthew 25:14-28 KJV)

14. For the kingdom of heaven is as a man travelling into a far country, who called his own servants, and delivered unto them his goods. 15. And unto one he gave five talents, to another two, and to another one; to every man according to his several ability; and straightway to his journey. 16. Then he that had received the five talents went and traded with the same, and made them other five talents. 17. And likewise he that had received two, he also gained other two. 18. But he that had received one went and digged in the earth, and hid his lord's money. 19. After a long time the lord of those servants cometh, and reckoneth with them. 20. And so he that had received five talents came brought other five talents, saying, Lord, thou deliveredst unto me five talents: behold, I have gained beside them five talents more. 21. His lord said unto him, Well done, thou good and faithful servant: thou hast been faithful over a few things, I will make thee ruler over many things: enter thou into the joy of thy lord. 22. He also that had received two talents came and said, Lord, thou deliveredst unto me two talents: behold, I have gained two other talents beside them. 23. His lord said unto him, Well done, good and faithful servant; thou hast been faithful over a few things, I will make thee ruler over many things: enter thou into the joy of thy lord. 24. Then he which had received the one talent came and said, Lord, I knew thee that thou art an hard man, reaping where thou hast not sown, and gathering where thou hast not strawed: 25. And I was afraid, and went and hid thy talent in the earth: lo, there thou has that is thine. 26. His lord

answered and said unto him, Thou wicked and slothful servant, thou knewest that I reap where I sowed not, and gather where I have not strawed: 27. Thou oughtest therefore to have put my money to the exchangers, and then at my coming I should receive mine own with usury. 28. Take therefore that talent from him, and give it unto him which hath ten talents.

Faithful service will be rewarded one day in Heaven. Jesus Himself will take great pleasure in rewarding His servants for their faithful service to Him. However it is important to remember that believers in Jesus Christ who have not served Jesus with their lives will suffer loss of reward. They could have had amazing rewards but chose to live their life of sin. Purity and good works will be rewarded and the pay off will be extraordinary. Focus on the Judgment Seat of Christ and the heavenly rewards, which Jesus will give to you for your faithful service. I have another verse, which talks about rewards in Heaven for faithfulness, which paints it in a more tangible and physical reward. Here is the verse.

(Luke 19:16-17 KJV)

16. Then came the first, saying, Lord, thy pound hath gained ten pounds. 17. And he said unto him, Well, thou good servant: because thou hast been faithful in a very little, have thou authority over ten cities.

Imagine being in charge of ten cities. Jesus will give authority to faithful servants and put them in charge of cities when we are back on the New Earth. So if you ever think about sinning or if you think that being faithful to Jesus won't matter. Then I want you to focus on the Judgment Seat of Christ and how Jesus will give you authority over cities just because you were faithful to Him. Ruling a city is a great honor so I think it would be more wise to resist temptation. Because which would you rather have; the fleeting pleasures of sin or the eternal leadership of a city? Only the good works we have done for Jesus after we get saved will be evaluated and rewarded at the Judgment Seat of Christ. The reason we will only be rewarded for the good works we have done for Jesus after we get saved is because before we got saved our good works were like filthy rags and they could not make an eternal significance. The reason they could not make an eternal significance is because they were not connected to Jesus Christ.

(Hebrews 11:24-26 KJV)

24. By faith Moses, when he was come to years, refused to be called the son of Pharaoh's daughter; 25. Choosing rather to suffer affliction with the people of God, than to enjoy the pleasures of sin for a season; 26. Esteeming the reproach of Christ greater riches than the treasures in Egypt: for he had respect unto the recompence of the reward.

Any eternal reward in Heaven is far better and greater than any sin this world has to offer. Moses chose the better thing. He chose not to give in to sin but to honor the Lord Jesus Christ. Because Moses chose to resist sin; one day the Lord Jesus Christ will reward Moses with a great eternal reward. If we could just get our eyes off this temporary and fleeting world of sin and keep our focus on Heaven and the eternal reward Jesus has promised his faithful followers; then I believe there would be Christians who would have a joy and happiness in the Lord. We would not be living for ourselves but we would be living for Jesus Christ. I don't want to compromise my walk with the Lord for a few minutes of pleasure of sin. All the pleasure of sin just gives us guilt, shame, regret, and pain.

I want to run my race well for Jesus Christ. I want to pass the finish line with a reward in my hand. I also want to fight the good fight so I can please Jesus and be rewarded by Him.

(2 Timothy 4:7-8 KJV)

7. I have fought a good fight, I have finished my course, I have kept the faith: 8. Henceforth there is laid up for me a crown of righteousness, which the Lord, the righteous judge, shall give me at that day: and not to me only, but unto all them also that love his appearing.

(1 Corinthians 9:24-25 KJV)

24. Know ye not that they which run in a race run all, but one receiveth the prize? So run, that ye may obtain. 25. And every man that striveth for the mastery is temperate in all things. Now they do it to obtain a corruptible crown; but we an incorruptible.

Imagine the Day of the Judgment Seat of Christ when Jesus Christ gives you the Crown of Righteousness and He also gives you the Incorruptible Crown. Imagine the moment when Jesus places the crowns on your head. After Jesus places the crowns on your head you see Him smile with the biggest smile ever. At that moment you now realize that He is pleased with you and that He is happy with the way that you lived your life for Him.

(Hebrews 12:1-2 KJV)

1. Wherefore seeing we also are compassed about with so great a cloud of witnesses, let us lay aside every weight, and the sin which doth so easily beset us, and let us run with patience the race that is set before us, 2. Looking unto Jesus the author and finisher of our faith; who for the joy that was set before him endured the cross, despising the shame, and is set down at the right hand of the throne of God.

We should run our race for Jesus Christ in such a way that Jesus will reward us for the way that we lived for Him. We should also keep in mind that Jesus is always watching us but also that there is a great cloud of witnesses in Heaven that watch us as well. They are cheering us on as we continue our race of faithfulness to Jesus Christ. I love this verse because it says how we are supposed to run our race. We are to get rid of the sin in our lives that so easily controls us. For example if the sin that so easily controls you is drinking alcohol. Then you should not go into a place that sells alcohol. Stay away from the liquor stores.

Or if your sin is lying then make it an effort to start telling the truth from now on. Or if your sin is looking at Pornography then buy some software that will block those pornography sites. Some people might say that it is legalism to be this radical for Jesus. But when it comes to the approval of Jesus and an eternal reward for yourself. Wouldn't you want to make every effort to please Jesus and to be rewarded for your faithfulness to Him? The only way we can run our race for Jesus Christ well is if we keep our eyes on Jesus every single day.

I find it very interesting that the verse says that Jesus Christ was looking for the joy that was set before Him. In other words Jesus was looking forward to His reward. Do you want to know what that reward is? Let's look at a Bible verse that will tell us the answer.

(Revelation 3:21 KJV)

21. To him that overcometh will I grant to sit with me in my throne, even as I also overcame, and am set down with my Father in his throne.

Jesus Christ endured being crucified on the cross and dieing to save sinners like you and me. The reward that Jesus was looking forward to; which kept Him going was that He would be able to sit on His Father's throne. Jesus desired honor and glory. With everything that Jesus went through while He was being crucified; I'm glad that Jesus Christ is being rewarded for what He did for us. Jesus Christ is now called the King of kings. Jesus overcame Death, Hell, Sin, and Satan. Because Jesus overcame those things He was able to sit down on God's Throne because Jesus was worthy. Look at the verse below and see the glory that God the Father gave to His Son Jesus Christ.

(Philippians 2:5-11 KJV)

5. Let this mind be in you, which was also in Christ Jesus: 6. Who, being in the form of God, thought it not robbery to be equal with God: 7. But made himself of no reputation, and took upon him the form of a servant, and was made in the likeness of men: 8. And being found in fashion as a man, he humbled himself, and

became obedient unto death, even the death of the cross. 9. Wherefore God also hath highly exalted him, and given him a name which is above every name: 10. That at the name of Jesus every knee should bow, of things in heaven, and things in earth, and things under the earth; 11. And that every tongue should confess that Jesus Christ is Lord, to the glory of God the Father.

So picture this. Let's use our imagination a little bit. On the day that we stand before the Judgment Seat of Christ we will see Jesus sitting on His throne looking down at us.

He then speaks to us and says, "I shall now judge the works which you have done for Me. Are you ready?"

You nod your head at Him and say, "Yes King Jesus I'm ready."

Jesus then names the good work, which you have done for Him. He then might ask an angel to bring the good work in and place it in the middle of the throne room between you and Jesus. The good work might be in a physical form which would go with Scripture that we just read in 1 Corinthians 3:10-15. Then fire would descend upon the good work to see what kind of good work it truly was. Was it a good work, which we did for Jesus Christ alone, or was it a good work, which we did to get praise from other people? After the fire has been quenched you would then see your good work still there as solid gold. Because your good work survived the fire Jesus will then give you a reward.

What that reward will be I have no clue at all. But if I had to guess I believe the reward would be something that you would enjoy personally. Maybe it is something that you have always wanted when you lived here on Earth but you could never attain or accomplish it. At that moment Jesus would give you that thing you have always dreamed of as your own personal reward. I'm excited when I think about the Judgment Seat of Christ. I hope you are excited to see Jesus at the Judgment Seat of Christ as well.

Now if the Judgment Seat of Christ still scares you. Then I want you to see this verse. This Bible verse brings comfort to me as I think about standing before Jesus on the Day of the Judgment Seat of Christ. Here is the verse.

(1 John 3:19-20 KJV)

19. And hereby we know that we are of the truth, and shall assure our hearts before him. 20. For if our heart condemn us, God is greater than our heart, and knoweth all things.

When you stand before Jesus at the Judgment Seat of Christ you may feel guilty for the things you have done. You may feel like you did nothing of eternal significance for Jesus. But here is the best part. Jesus has a better memory than you do. In fact Jesus knows everything.

(1 Corinthians 4:5 KJV)

5. Therefore judge nothing before the time, until the Lord come, who both will bring to light the hidden things of darkness, and will make manifest the counsels of the hearts: and then shall every man have praise of God.

Jesus will find something in your life that deserves a reward. Take comfort in that truth. Jesus will praise you for all of your sacrifice, devotion, and love towards Him. All of those times when you gave money to someone and no one else knew about it. Jesus saw that and He will reward you for it. All of those times when you prayed by yourself and no else knew about it. Jesus will gladly reward you for your devotion to Him. All of those times when you felt unappreciated for all of your hard work for Jesus. Jesus is watching and He will reward you publicly and it will bring great pleasure to Him. I would like to show you a verse because without this verse then there is no chance of us getting rewards. Jesus rewards us for our faithfulness to Him. So if Jesus rewards us for faithfulness then that means we need to be faithful to Him. Here is the verse.

(1 Corinthians 4:2 KJV)

2. Moreover it is required in stewards,
that a man be found faithful.

We are stewards of what God has given us. God owns it all. God owns all of our money and possessions. God is just letting us use it. He wants us to use the things that He has given us for the glory of His name. Since Jesus gave us everything we have in the first place; we need to make it our top priority to use what Jesus has given to us to advance His Heavenly Kingdom. You can advance His heavenly kingdom by tithing to your church, buying Bibles for people, giving to people in need, buy tracts for people so that the gospel is being spread across the Earth, and there are many other ways to advance His Heavenly Kingdom. Those are just a few of them. Jesus will reward you for you helping to advance His Heavenly Kingdom. Jesus will judge us by the very resources that Jesus has entrusted to us. So we need to make it our top priority to remain faithful to Him. Pray to Jesus that He will give you more opportunities to be faithful to Him. Jesus will gladly answer that prayer and one day He will reward you for that very act of faithfulness, which you did for Him.

I would like to end this chapter with a final Bible verse. I believe this Bible verse will encourage you as you stand before Jesus at the Judgment Seat of Christ. Here is the verse.

(1 Corinthians 3:6-8 KJV)

6. I have planted, Apollos watered; but God gave the increase. 7. So then neither is he that planteth any thing, neither he that watereth; but God that giveth the increase. 8. Now he that planteth and he that watereth are one: and every man shall receive his own reward according to his own labour.

I find this verse very comforting because this verse is saying that it is not up to us to handle the results. It is up to God to handle the results. When you share the gospel with someone you are planting a seed in that person, or you may be watering that person, or perhaps you shall reap and that person gets saved. But just remember that it was not you who caused that person to be saved it was God who touched that person's heart through His Holy Spirit that caused that person to want to be saved.

At the Judgment Seat of Christ; Jesus will not be looking for huge results from you. Since the results are up to God in the first place. All Jesus is looking for is if you were willing to share the gospel with people. Were you willing to invest your time, your money, and your energy in other people's lives? Were you willing to help people come to know their Savior Jesus Christ? That is what Jesus will be looking for. People matter to Jesus because people are eternal. When you take the time to invest in another person by explaining the gospel to them so that they see their desperate need for Jesus Christ to save them; that catches Jesus Christ's attention because you are making an eternal difference.

When you are investing in other people because you want to please Jesus that has eternal significance. Investing in people is the only thing that has eternal significance. Jesus will reward you for every time you have shared the gospel with someone. You can make an eternal difference in people's lives by just inviting them to church. Or you can make an eternal difference by sharing the gospel with them. Or you can make an eternal difference by giving them a gospel tract. There are many other ways but those are the most helpful.

CHAPTER **10**

BEING WITH JESUS IN HEAVEN!

Heaven is not Heaven without Jesus being there. Jesus is the main person that you will always want to see and talk with for all of eternity. I'm so excited to see Jesus in Heaven. I know that Jesus feels the same way about me. Jesus is excited to see you in Heaven too. He can't wait until He can wrap His arms around you and tell you how much He loves you and how much you mean to Him. Here is a verse that talks about what Jesus will be doing for us in Heaven to show us how much He loves us. Here is the verse.

(Ephesians 2:6-7 KJV)

6. And hath raised us up together, and made us sit together in heavenly places in Christ Jesus: 7. That in the ages to come he might shew the exceeding riches of his grace in his kindness toward us through Christ Jesus.

Throughout all of eternity when we are in Heaven; Jesus will continue to express His kindness towards us. He will always show us His kindness by how He talks to us, how He treats us, and by Jesus always reminding us that He is happy that we are with Him in Heaven. Jesus might even point to the marks in His hands and His feet to continuously remind us the great depth of His love for us. I believe every time that I see Jesus in Heaven I will bow down before Him and feel so unworthy to be in His presence. Because I know what kind of person I truly am. I will feel like I don't deserve Jesus or Heaven. But the best part is that because Jesus knows what I'll be thinking in my heart that He will come over to me. He will pick me up off from the ground, He will look deep in my eyes and He will then hug me with ultimate acceptance, kindness, and love.

Finally Jesus will say to me, "Nick, I love you completely. I know all about what you did on Earth and I still had an eternal and undying love for you Nick. I want you to know that none of that can change My love for you. I want you here in Heaven with Me. I know you feel like if you had not sinned that you would feel worthy to be in My presence but remember you can't earn your way to Heaven. It is by My grace and by My love for you that you are here in Heaven with Me."

Just insert your name in the paragraph up above and imagine Jesus saying that to you. I believe Jesus will share intimate moments with every person in Heaven. No one in Heaven will ever feel unloved by Jesus. Everyone in Heaven will be filled with love because they know how much Jesus loves them personally. Imagine talking to Jesus about things that you had prayed to Jesus about while you were living on Earth before you died. You and Jesus are having a wonderful conversation basically talking about the goodness of God in your life. You will be talking to the Creator who created human beings, the animals, and the entire universe. But more specifically you will be talking with the One who created you and made you. You can ask Jesus about anything about your life and why those things happened to you; and Jesus will give you the answer you have been searching for your entire life.

You can ask Jesus why He made you with your specific personality. Why He made you like certain things. You can ask Him why you like certain kinds of music, food, books, and movies. For me personally I want to ask Jesus why I love superheroes so much. Jesus is the One who made me so if anyone knows that answer it has to be Jesus Christ Himself. You will be able to talk to Jesus about anything that happened in your life and He will listen to you with His full and undivided attention. You can talk to Jesus about your failures, your disappointments, and your dreams. Jesus will be right there listening to you as you speak. He will have sympathy for you and He will have empathy for you. Because Jesus is the One who created you He will be the only person who truly understands how you feel. I hope you are excited to meet with, talk with, have fun with, and be with Jesus in Heaven.

Chapter 11

Good works for Jesus!

Before we can do good works for Jesus it is important for us to know why we should do good works in the first place. If we don't have a reason why we should do good works then we will have no hope in us doing a lifetime of good works for Jesus. So let us explore some Scripture that explain why we should do good works. The first reason is that we should do good works to glorify God.

(Matthew 5:16 KJV)

16. Let your light so shine before men, that they may see your good works, and glorify your Father which is in heaven.

We should not do good works to glorify ourselves or to get praise from men and women. How many people have done good works to get praise from men and women only to discover that they get angry, sad, or depressed when they don't receive the recognition for their good deeds from those people? The problem isn't us desiring praise. The problem is when we seek praise from people instead of praise from God. There are two bible verses that express when God will praise us and give us honor. I would like to show you those verses right now.

(John 12:43 KJV)

43. For they loved the praise of men more than the praise of God.

(1 Corinthians 4:5 KJV)

5. Therefore judge nothing before the time, until the Lord come, who both will bring to light the hidden things of darkness, and will make manifest the counsels of the hearts: and then shall every man have praise of God.

God will one day thank us for all of the good things we have done for Him. The Creator, King, Savior, Lord, and God of the entire universe will personally thank you one day for the tiniest good deeds that you have done for Him even when you probably thought that those things did not matter. You will also be rewarded for the enormous good deeds that you have done to show your devotion to Jesus. I believe God will give us His approval of our good deeds towards us at the Judgment Seat of Christ. Think about your Creator and your Savior Jesus Christ showing His approval of your entire life. Then He will personally thank you for all the good things you have done for His name. When you think about that; why would you want anyone else's approval? The praise from men is fleeting and temporary. The praise from God is lasting and eternal. Here is a verse that explains that Jesus is watching us when we give to people in need. Even the smallest act of kindness will be rewarded. Here is the verse.

(Mark 9:41 KJV)

41. For whosoever shall give you a cup of water to drink in my name, because ye belong to Christ, verily I say unto you, he shall not lose his reward.

Every time you give something to someone in need be encouraged that one day you will be rewarded publicly by Jesus Himself. As you give to people you are storing up treasures and rewards in Heaven which will be given to you at the Judgment Seat of Christ. Don't do good works to be rewarded by men but do good works to be rewarded by God. The second reason we should do good works is because we were created by God to do good works after we get saved. Here is the verse.

(Ephesians 2:8-10 KJV)

8. For by grace are ye saved through faith; and that not of yourselves: it is the gift of God: 9. Not of works, lest any man should boast. 10. For we are his workmanship, created in Christ Jesus unto good works, which God hath before ordained that we should walk in them.

How exciting it is that we get to do good works for Jesus Christ for the rest of our life and then Jesus will reward us. As you live out each day look for new ways that you can do good works for Jesus.

You can do good works like encouraging someone, sharing the gospel with someone, giving someone money, possibly making someone a meal to eat, praying for someone, teaching someone the Word of God, and giving gifts to people. Finally we should look for ways to encourage each other to do good works. So why would we encourage each other to do good works you might ask? Well the main reason is because the Bible tells us that we should help each other and to encourage one another to do good works. The second reason is that we should desire for other people to get as many heavenly rewards as they possibly can. Here is the verse.

(Hebrews 10:24 KJV)

24. And let us consider one another to provoke unto love and to good works:

Good works do not happen automatically. We need to be encouraged to help us do good works for Jesus. Perhaps the encouragement that will help us do good works may be listening to a sermon on the topic of good works, or reading a book on the topic of the Judgment Seat of Christ. Or perhaps it is a brother and sister in Christ who encourages us to keep on doing our good works for Jesus because they know that Jesus will reward us for our good works. I would like to show you a Bible verse to encourage you to not give up in doing good works for Jesus. For in the end you will be rewarded by Jesus. Here is the verse.

(Galatians 6:9 KJV)

9. And let us not be weary in well doing: for in due season we shall reap, if we faint not.

I will not lie to you. Life is tough. At times life can be incredibly depressing and discouraging. There will be times in your life that will cause immense stress and anxiety. The darkest moments in your life when you feel like giving up in doing good is the exact moment when you need to keep on going in doing good. If you keep on doing good eventually you will blessed for doing that. That is not my words saying that. It is God's Word saying that and that is a promise from God Himself.

I have a final Bible verse to show you on why it is important for us to do good works. Here is the verse.

(James 2:14-18 and 26 KJV)

14. What doth it profit, my brethren, though a man say he hath faith, and have not works? can faith save him? 15. If a brother or sister be naked, and destitute of daily food, 16. And one of you say unto them, Depart in peace, be ye warmed and filled; notwithstanding ye give them not those things which are needful to the body; what doth it profit? 17. Even so faith, if it hath not works is dead, being alone. 18. Yea, a man may say, Thou hast faith, and I have works: shew me thy faith without thy works, and I will shew thee my faith by my works. 26. For as the body without the spirit is dead, so faith without works is dead also.

If we are truly saved people who are genuine believers in Jesus Christ then we will have good works flowing out of us by the way that we live. We will want to help the less fortunate people. We will want to give. We'll want to share the gospel with people. We will think of others more than we think of ourselves. We will do good works on a consistent and increasing daily basis. Our good works will keep increasing that it will become natural for us to do good works for Jesus and other people. Forgiven people who are saved will want to express their gratitude to Jesus Christ by doing good works for Him.

CHAPTER 12

SERVING GOD AND OTHERS!

As we serve God we will undoubtedly begin to start serving others. It is impossible to serve God without having a burning passion and desire to want to serve others. As we look for ways to serve God it will always include a way to serve people. Let's say a person wants to serve God in church by teaching kid's ministry. They are serving God but also in the process they are serving the children. Or let's say a person wants to serve God by cleaning the church. They are serving God by cleaning the church but they are also serving others because in the process the church is clean for the people of God to enjoy.

Or let's say a person wants to serve God by giving their money to a Christian charity. They are serving God because they gave their money to a Christian charity and in the process they are serving others because the money blesses the people and the gospel is being preached to them. I would like to show you some Bible verses about serving God but also verses about serving others. I pray that these verses encourage you as you serve God and as you serve others.

(Matthew 6:24 KJV)

24. No man can serve two masters: for either he will hate the one, and love the other; or else he will hold to the one, and despise the other. Ye cannot serve God and mammon.

I started off with serving God with this verse because if we are not willing to serve God with our money then it will be more difficult for us to truly serve God. Mammon is another word for money.

Jesus wants every area of our lives to be devoted to Him and that includes the money that He has graciously entrusted to us. Remember we are stewards of God's money. A steward is someone who is entrusted to manage someone else's possessions.

Since God owns all the money in the world that means that even if we work for our money it ultimately belongs to God. Here is a verse that talks about how God owns the wealth of the world.

(Haggai 2:8 KJV)

8. The silver is mine, and the gold is mine,
saith the LORD of hosts.

God is basically calling us stewards because He is allowing us to manage His money and He is watching us to see what we will do with His money. If we are faithful with His money on planet Earth then when we get to Heaven we will be entrusted with the true riches of Heaven. Here is the verse when Jesus speaks about the true riches of Heaven.

(Luke 16:11-12 KJV)

11. If therefore ye have not been faithful in the unrighteous mammon who will commit to your trust the true riches? 12. And if ye have not been faithful in that which is another man's, who shall give you that which is your own?

Unrighteous mammon is also another word for earthly money. It is called unrighteous mammon because money can be used for unrighteous things. As we are faithful and wise in how we use God's money; one day Jesus will give us true riches in Heaven. And I believe when it talks about if you have not been faithful in that which is another man's. I believe the word "another man's" is speaking about Jesus Christ. We should be faithful with God's money because Jesus put us in charge of managing His money. The good news is that if we are faithful to Jesus with the money He has entrusted us while on planet Earth that one day Jesus will give us something that belongs to us in Heaven. It is right there in text. It says who shall give you that which is your own? In other words you will have personal property that belongs to you in Heaven. So you may be asking yourself how can I be faithful to God with the money He has given me? Here is the verse.

(Proverbs 3:9-10 KJV)

9. Honour the LORD with thy substance, and with the firstfruits of all thine increase: 10. So shall thy barns be filled with plenty, and thy presses shall burst out with new wine.

As we give to the Lord we are honoring Him. As we give to God He gives it right back to us. God is a generous God. And when it says firstfruits that just means that we give the first 10 percent of our paychecks to God in our tithes to the church. We should be giving the first 10 percent of our paycheck as soon as we receive it. We don't wait to give our 10 percent after we pay off our bills. We give Jesus our 10 percent before we even spend a single cent. One thing we can do to make sure God is the first priority in our life is for us to give our tithe first; before we spend anything. Here is another verse that talks about tithes and offerings.

(Malachi 3:8 KJV)

8. Will a man rob God? Yet ye have robbed me. But ye say, Wherein have we robbed thee? In tithes and offerings.

As we are faithful with our tithes and free will offerings we are being faithful to God. God is taking note how faithful we are to Him with His money. One day Jesus will give us our reward for being faithful to Him with the money He has entrusted us. Now you may be asking why must I be a steward who is faithful to God? Here is the verse to answer that question.

(1 Corinthians 4:2 KJV)

3. Moreover it is required in stewards,
that a man be found faithful.

God says in His Word that as stewards we must be faithful to Him. Because God makes the rules we are to live by them. Now I would like to show you some Bible verses about serving God but in the process you are also serving people as well. Here are some verses.

(Hebrews 6:10 KJV)

10. For God is not unrighteous to forget your work and labour of love, which ye have shewed toward his name, in that ye have ministered to the saints, and do minister.

God will not forget your hard work and labor, which you have done for Him out of love for Him. As you are serving and helping your fellow believers in Jesus Christ at your local church; God is paying careful attention to detail. Your hard work for God and others will not be in vain. Your faithful service to God and others will count and it will last for all of eternity. It will not be forgotten. Here is another verse.

(Philippians 2:3-5 KJV)

3. Let nothing be done through strife or vainglory; but in lowliness of mind let each esteem other better than themselves. 4. Look not every man on his own things, but every man also on the things of others. 5. Let this mind be in you, which was also in Christ Jesus:

We are to treat other people better than we treat ourselves. For example let's say you are about to buy a great amount of groceries while you are in the waiting line but you see someone up ahead of you that can't pay for their groceries. By treating others better than yourself you would offer to pay for their groceries. You might need to put some stuff back from your grocery cart but in the end you are acting like Christ, which is way more important than a few more groceries. As you treat other people and focus on other people as more important than yourself you are using the same mindset or the same mind that was in Christ Jesus. I would like to show you a verse that talks about Jesus Christ's mindset when He was here on Earth. Jesus Christ spoke this verse about Himself. Here is the verse.

(Mark 10:45 KJV)

45. For even the Son of man came not to be ministered unto, but to minister, and to give his life a ransom for many.

Jesus was focused on others and He wanted to help them as much as He could. He showed that He cared for them by healing the sick, opening the eyes of the blind, and He multiplied the bread and fish to feed a multitude of people. Jesus had compassion for the multitude because they had stayed to listen to Him speak even though they had not eaten for three days. Finally to show how much He cared about other people more than Himself. He chose to die on a cross so that we would not have to go to Hell and so that we could go to Heaven to live with Jesus forever.

Jesus could have chosen not to go the Cross and be completely justified in His ways. God does not owe us anything. We deserve eternal punishment in Hell but Jesus cared for, loved us, and had compassion on us that He did not want that to happen to us. So in the ultimate act of love He shed His blood for us that we might be saved. Jesus cared about other people and so should we. Jesus gave His life for people and so should we. Jesus comforted people who needed comforting and so should we.

Be like Jesus and start to help people who are in need. It puts a smile on Jesus Christ's face when He sees you help someone who needs to be comforted. It could be something simple as writing an encouraging letter. It does not have to be extravagant or expensive just something simple. But if you want to do something extravagant or expensive for someone else that is fine as well. We have freedom in Jesus Christ to help people in need whether that is something simple or something extravagant. It is a joy to serve God and people. Here is another verse.

(Galatians 5:13 KJV)

13. For, brethren, ye have been called unto liberty; only use not liberty for an occasion to the flesh,
but by love serve one another.

We should not use our freedom in Christ to satisfy our sinful desires. Instead we should use our freedom in Christ to serve people with our overflowing love for Jesus Christ. Some people believe that if people knew the grace, forgiveness, and freedom in Christ that Jesus offers us; that we would just sin like crazy. They believe that people would misuse the grace of God. I whole-heartedly disagree with that belief. I believe that if people truly understood the fullest extent of what Jesus has done for them that they would have a completely different outlook on life and how they view their sin.

I believe that people who misuse the grace of God don't truly understand the grace of God. Then there are people who treat the grace of God as sacred, holy, and who also have a thankful heart for God's grace in their life. These are the people who truly understand the grace of God. Jesus spoke these words in the Bible verse below.

(Luke 7:47 KJV)

47. Wherefore I say unto thee, Her sins, which are many, are forgiven; for she loved much: but to whom little is forgiven, the same loveth little.

People who have been forgiven of their few sins only love a little. It is evident by how they love and live. However people who have committed many sins and have realized that Jesus Christ has forgiven them all of their sins will love a lot. They decide to express their overflowing gratitude and thankfulness to Jesus in the form of loving God and loving other people extraordinarily. Love is bubbling up inside of their hearts and they have a deep desire to express their love to God by serving others. Because keeping that love inside them would be impossible to contain.

CHAPTER 13

LIFE ON THE NEW HEAVENS AND THE NEW EARTH!

Now we have come to the most important part of this book. We shall see in Scripture what life will be like for us on the New Heaven and the New Earth. What makes Heaven and Earth so glorious is that after the first Heaven and the first Earth have passed away; God will make a New Heaven and a New Earth. You see as Christians we have the hope that we will come back to live on Planet Earth again. We call this the New Earth. We will inherit the New Earth and rule it with Jesus Christ. It is God's desire that we pick up where we left off. In the beginning God put us in charge of taking care of the animals and to also take care of and rule Planet Earth to the glory of God. Here is the verse that explains God's original design for us which God wanted us to accomplish with the Earth. Here is the verse.

(Genesis 1:28 KJV)

28. And God blessed them, and God said unto them, Be fruitful, and multiply, and replenish the earth, and subdue it: and have dominion over the fish of the sea, and over the fowl of the air, and over every living thing that moveth upon the earth.

We as Christians who love planet Earth don't have to say goodbye to the Earth as we die and go to Heaven. We can have confidence that Jesus will bring us back to the Earth to rule and reign with Him. The New Heaven will come down on the New Earth and the two will become one. No longer will there be separation from

Heaven and Earth. No longer will there be separation from God and men. Now I would like to show you an Old Testament passage, which specifically talks about the New Heavens and the New Earth just in case you thought that it only spoke about the New Heavens and the New Earth in the New Testament. This passage is found in the book of Isaiah. This is God speaking about creating the New Heavens and the New Earth. Here is the verse.

(Isaiah 65:17-25 KJV)

17. For, behold, I create new heavens and a new earth: and the former shall not be remembered, nor come into mind. 18. But be ye glad and rejoice for ever in that which I create: for, behold, I create Jerusalem a rejoicing, and her people a joy. 19. And I will rejoice in Jerusalem, and joy in my people: and the voice of weeping shall be no more heard in her, nor the voice of crying. 20. There shall be no more thence an infant of days, nor an old man that hath not filled his days: for the child shall die an hundred years old; but the sinner being an hundred shall be accursed. 21. And they shall build houses, and inhabit them; and they shall plant vineyards, and eat the fruit of them. 22. They shall not build, and another inhabit; they shall not plant, and another eat: for as the days of a tree are the days of my people, and mine elect shall long enjoy the work of their hands. 23. They shall not labour in vain, nor bring forth for trouble; for they are the seed of the blessed of the LORD, and their offspring with them. 24. And it shall comes to pass, that before they call, I will answer; and while they are yet speaking I will hear. 25. The wolf and the lamb shall feed together, and the lion shall eat straw like the bullock: and dust shall be the serpent's meat. They shall not hurt nor destroy in all my holy mountain, saith the LORD.

It is amazing to see what God has in store for us. We shall be joyful in the presence of God. No longer will we be depressed. As a person who struggles with depression I find comfort in the happiness of Heaven. If you are a person who struggles with depression know that Jesus wants to give you hope and to help you have a correct perspective about your life. Right now life on Earth is difficult for us. The lie that we so easily believe is that our life will always be difficult and that our life will never get any better. The truth is that Jesus has great plans for us. The cool thing about the New Heaven and the New Earth is that animals will not kill other animals and they will not kill humans. That is amazing and I can't wait to see that on the New Earth. If there is a person who is struggling with sin and depression then I would like to share a verse that has brought so much comfort to me. I hope it brings comfort to you. Here is the verse.

(Job 11:13-19 KJV)

13. If thou prepare thine heart, and stretch out thine hands toward him; 14. If iniquity be in thine hand, put it far away, and let not wickedness dwell in thy tabernacles. 15. For then shalt thou lift up thy face without spot; yea, thou shalt be stedfast, and shall not fear: 16. Because thou shalt forget thy misery, and remember it as waters that pass away: 17. And thine age shall be clearer than the noonday: thou shalt shine forth, thou shalt be as the morning. 18. And thou shalt be secure, because there is hope; yea, thou shalt dig about thee, and thou shalt take thy rest in safety. 19. Also thou shalt lie down, and none shall make thee afraid; yea, many shall make suit unto thee.

Basically this verse is saying that if we repent of our sins then we will forget our misery. We won't be ridden with guilt, regret, misery, anger, or sadness over our sin because we have repented of our sins and are not going back to that lifestyle of sin. We will have hope because God promises us hope. And what is that hope? That hope is Jesus and Heaven.

Our life should shine brightly for Jesus. The light of Jesus in our life will only be bright after we have extinguished the darkness that has been lurking in our lives for so many years. As we repent and reject our old lifestyle of sin then other people will see the light in us and will want to know what has caused this great transformation in our lives. And the answer to that question would be that Jesus is the one who is responsible for this great transformation in our lives. I would like to show you another verse in the Bible that talks about the New Heaven and the New Earth it is found in the book of Isaiah in the Old Testament. Here is the verse.

(Isaiah 60:19-22 KJV)

19. The sun shall be no more thy light by day; neither for brightness shall the moon give light unto thee: but the LORD shall be unto thee an everlasting light, and thy God thy glory. 20. Thy sun shall no more go down; neither shall thy moon withdraw itself: for the LORD shall be thine everlasting light, and the days of thy mourning shall be ended. 21. Thy people also shall be all righteous: they shall inherit the land for ever, the branch of my planting the work of my hands, that I may be glorified. 22. A little one shall become a thousand, and a small one a strong nation: I the LORD will hasten it in his time.

The verse above speaks about the kind of condition the New Earth will be like and the condition of God's people. It says that God will be an everlasting light. God will always shine the brightest on the New Earth. God is the source of light and He gives His people light. God gives us spiritual light and in this portion of Scripture it says that God will give us physical light from His very being when we are on the New Earth. It also says that God's people will be righteous and that their mourning shall end. Which means that there will be no more tears when we are on the New Earth. I would like to show you another verse, which ties into the verse above. The verse is found in the book of Revelation. Here is the verse.

(Revelation 21:23-25 KJV)

23. And the city had no need of the sun, neither of the moon, to shine in it: for the glory of God did lighten it, and the Lamb is the light thereof. 24. And the nations of them which are saved shall walk in the light of it: and the kings of the earth do bring their glory and honour into it. 25. And the gates of it shall not be shut at all by day: for there shall be no night there.

There will be no night on the New Earth. Scripture is very clear when it says in Revelation 21:25 that there shall be no night there. When it says the Lamb is the light that is speaking about Jesus Christ. Since Jesus is God then it makes sense that the book of Isaiah says that God will be an everlasting light.

I like that there will be no night on the New Earth because a lot of bad things happen in the night. Think about all the murders, thefts, and car accidents which happen at night. Plus what time of day are people most scared during the entire day? The answer is night time. Jesus will take away the fear of night by removing the night altogether. I would like to show you another verse which speaks about the New Heaven and the New Earth and what kind of people we should be. Here is the verse.

(2 Peter 3:13-14 KJV)

13. Nevertheless we, according to his promise, look for new heavens and a new earth, wherein dwelleth righteousness. 14. Wherefore, beloved, seeing that ye look for such things, be diligent that ye may be found of him in peace, without spot, and blameless.

Because we have such a great promise from God that He will make a New Heavens and a New Earth we should focus on living a righteous life before the eyes of God. God is always watching us. He is the Audience of One. When we see Jesus we want to be without spot, be blameless, and be found of Him in peace. So how do we get blameless, without spot, and found of Him in peace? Well if there is sin in our life which we have not repented of then the first thing we should do is repent of that sin and make it our goal to no longer go back to that sin. Our conscience will become clean because we are no longer doing the sin, which caused us to feel dirty in the past. So in that way we shall be without spot or in other words we shall be clean.

Now I would like to show you the good news and glorious beauty about the New Heavens and the New Earth. But before we can discuss about all the beauty of the New Earth we should discuss the horrible thing about the Curse of the Earth. Here is the verse.

(Genesis 3:17 KJV)

17. And unto Adam he said, Because thou hast hearkened unto the voice of thy wife, and hast eaten of the tree, of which I commanded thee, saying, Thou shalt not eat of it: cursed is the ground for thy sake; in sorrow shalt thou eat of it
all the days of thy life;

You see in the beginning God created the Heavens and the Earth. He then created Adam and Eve as the first two human beings. He let them eat of every tree in the garden of Eden except from the tree of knowledge of good and evil. But they sinned and ate from the tree of knowledge of good and evil. Because of their sin God cursed the Earth as described in the verse above. The great thing about God is that one day He is going to create a New Earth and a New Heavens and the Curse will be gone forever. The New Earth will be beyond description of pure beauty. It will be glorious. The New Heavens and the New Earth will be glorious in beauty and wonder. So now let's look at some verses about the New Earth and the New Heavens.

(Revelation 22:3-5 KJV)

3. And there shall be no more curse: but the throne of God and of the Lamb shall be in it; and his servants shall serve him: 4. And they shall see his face; and his name shall be in their foreheads. 5. And there shall be no night there; and they need no candle, neither light of the sun; for the Lord God giveth them light: and they shall reign for ever and ever.

So as you can see from this verse the Curse of the Earth will be removed which is a very good thing for us. The New Earth will not have the Curse so that means that we will get to see an even more beautiful New Earth than we could ever imagine. Also the part that should make us excited is the fact that one day God will put His name on our foreheads. By God putting His name on our foreheads God is saying to us and showing us in a very realistic way that we belong to Him, which is the greatest honor ever. Think about that for a moment. The Greatest Being in the entire universe, who in fact created the entire universe and who also created everything in it, which includes you also; is one day going to put His name on your forehead and that is something that should definitely put a smile on your face.

What I find fascinating is that there will be no night there on the New Earth. The fact that we won't need the sun to shine light for us is mind boggling. What is amazing is that Jesus will be the light for us. Now as for me and you who are familiar with the sun giving us light on planet Earth. It will definitely be quite an adjustment for us to get used to on the New Earth. Instead of the sun giving us light Jesus will give us light. Here is the verse that explains Jesus being the light for us on the New Earth.

(Revelation 21:23-24 KJV)

23. And the city had no need of the sun, neither of the moon, to shine in it: for the glory of God did lighten it, and the Lamb is the light thereof. 24. And the nations of them which are saved shall walk in the light of it: and the kings of the earth do bring their glory and honour into it.

The Lamb is Jesus Christ. So Jesus Christ is the One responsible for giving light to the whole world. Think about how glorious Jesus will look like with all of this magnificent light coming out of Him. Jesus will truly be breathtaking and I can't wait to see Him. I hope you are getting excited about seeing Jesus as well. Jesus is the only one who deserves glory, praise, and honor. Remember that Scripture speaks about us reigning and ruling the New Earth with Jesus

Christ. Remember Jesus is called the King of kings. He is the ultimate King and He graciously allows us to rule with Him. We shall be kings and queens when we are back on the New Earth.

For me personally I believe that the glory and honor that it is speaking about concerning the kings of the New Earth in Revelation 21:23-24 is that we will create things that bring glory to Jesus Christ and present them to Him as a way of worship towards Him. Jesus will then say to us that He is pleased with the work that we have done for Him. Then we will feel so much gratitude, love, admiration, and excitement towards Jesus that we can't wait to get home to work on the next project that will give Jesus honor and glory even more.

So what kind of things would we bring to Jesus on the New Earth that would give Him honor and glory towards His name? I believe it will be stuff that God has given to us in our natural talents. For example if you are talented in writing then you might write a great book that brings honor and glory to Jesus Christ. Or if you are a painter you might paint a masterpiece, which shows the beauty of God's creation. Or if you are a musician you might perform and write songs that declares God's goodness. You might be performing the song in front of Jesus while He is watching you play for Him. And you can bet that He will be smiling at you and He will be so happy to hear you use your gifts for His glory. There are many other gifts that can bring glory to God but those are just a few of them.

Now we shall talk about the Water of life that we will drink. And we shall talk about the Tree of Life that we will eat on the New Earth. Here is the verse.

(Revelation 22:1-3 KJV)

1. And he shewed me a pure river of water of life, clear as crystal, proceeding out of the throne of God and of the Lamb. 2. In the midst of the street of it, and on either side of the river, was there the tree of life, which bare twelve manner of fruits, and yielded her fruit every month: and the leaves of the tree were for the healing of the nations. 3. And there shall be no more curse: but the throne of God and of the Lamb shall be in it; and his servants shall serve him:

Imagine how beautiful the Water of Life will look like being as clear as crystal. Imagine how good it will taste to drink from the water that is truly life. Then imagine how majestic and glorious the Tree of Life will look like. Can you imagine how good the fruit will taste from the Tree of Life? The fruit will explode our taste buds beyond anything we could imagine. It will be the most amazing thing we have ever tasted before. There will be no more curse on the Earth. Finally as servants of God we will serve God. We shall now talk about what the city of God will look like on the New Earth.

(Revelation 21:2 KJV)

2. And I John saw the holy city, new Jerusalem, coming down
from God out of heaven, prepared as a bride
adorned for her husband.

God is preparing us this city because we are the Bride of Christ. Here are some other verses about what the city will look like.

(Revelation 21:10-14 KJV)

10. And he carried me away in the spirit to a great and high
mountain, and shewed me that great city, the holy Jerusalem,
descending out of heaven from God, 11. Having the glory of God:
and her light was like unto a stone most precious, even like a
jasper stone, clear as crystal; 12. And had a wall great and high,
and had twelve gates, and at the gates twelve angels, and names
written thereon, which are the names of the twelve tribes of the
children of Israel: 13. On the east three gates; on the north three
gates; on the south three gates; and on the west three gates.
14. And the wall of the city had twelve foundations,
and in them the names of the twelve apostles of the Lamb.

The city of God will be absolutely breathtaking. The twelve apostles will be given a great honor for their faithful service to Jesus. The twelve angels at every gate are to show that there is protection and safety on every side. God's people will live in safety and peace for all eternity. I have a verse that describes how glorious Heaven will be like on the New Earth. This verse will describe in great detail the beauty and glory of the heavenly city called the New Jerusalem on the New Earth.

(Revelation 21:18-21 KJV)

18. And the building of the wall of it was of jasper: and the city was pure gold, like unto clear glass. 19. And the foundations of the wall of the city were garnished with all manner of precious stones. The first foundation was jasper; the second, sapphire; the third, a chalcedony; the fourth, an emerald; 20. The fifth, sardonyx; the sixth, sardius; the seventh, chrysolyte; the eighth, beryl; the ninth, a topaz; the tenth, a chrysoprasus; the eleventh, a jacinth; the twelfth, an amethyst. 21. And the twelve gates were twelve pearls: every several gate was of one pearl: and the street of the city was pure gold, as it were transparent glass.

Think about seeing a gold city. The heavenly city will definitely take your breath away when you see it. How awesome will it be to walk on streets of gold? The New Heavens and the New Earth will be absolutely beautiful. The heavenly city the New Jerusalem will be dazzling and sparkling to look at with all of those precious stones. The city will be bright because of the gold covering the entire city and the light that comes from Jesus Christ.

What I find fascinating is that each gate will have one giant pearl on the gate. That is one big pearl. I have a verse that talks about us inheriting the kingdom of God. Here is the verse.

(James 2:5 KJV)

5. Hearken, my beloved brethren, Hath not God chosen the poor of this world rich in faith, and heirs of the kingdom which he hath promised to them that love him?

I like this verse a lot because it talks about how people who are poor in this world but are rich in faith will inherit the heavenly kingdom on the New Earth. The people who are in extreme poverty on this Earth are usually the ones who have great faith in God. They pray to Jesus for their provisions each day because all they have is their faith to depend on. Jesus is the person they depend on. One day you will be rich for all of eternity if you belong to Jesus Christ. The New Jerusalem heavenly city will be your inheritance from God. You will live in that city forever. Now I would like to show you a few Bible verses of us reigning with Jesus Christ.

(Daniel 7:18 KJV)

18. But the saints of the most High shall take the kingdom, and possess the kingdom for ever, even for ever and ever.

Think about that for a moment. We shall reign with Jesus Christ forever and ever on the New Earth. That is truly amazing and I can't quite wrap my mind around living forever but the Bible says that I will and I'm happy that I will live with Jesus forever. I hope you will be with Jesus forever and reign with Him on the New Earth as well. Here is another verse.

(Revelation 5:10 KJV)

10. And hast made us unto our God kings and priests: and we shall reign on the earth.

There has never been a greater honor than reigning with Jesus Christ on the New Earth forever. Reigning with Jesus is the most amazing, satisfying, rewarding, exciting, and fulfilling thing that we will ever experience on the New Earth. Now I would like to explain a verse that Jesus Christ Himself spoke concerning us. We will look at each of the blessings that Jesus spoke of. You probably know it as the Beatitudes or perhaps you have heard of it as the Sermon on the Mount. Here is the verse.

(Matthew 5:2-12 KJV)

2. And he opened his mouth, and taught them saying, 3. Blessed are the poor in spirit: for theirs is the kingdom of heaven. 4. Blessed are they that mourn: for they shall be comforted. 5. Blessed are the meek: for they shall inherit the earth. 6. Blessed are they which do hunger and thirst after righteousness: for they shall be filled. 7. Blessed are the merciful: for they shall obtain mercy. 8. Blessed are the pure in heart: for they shall see God. 9. Blessed are the peacemakers: for they shall be called the children of God. 10. Blessed are they which are persecuted for righteousness' sake: for theirs is the kingdom of heaven. 11. Blessed are ye, when men shall revile you, and persecute you, and shall say all manner of evil against you falsely, for my sake. 12. Rejoice, and be exceeding glad: for great is your reward in heaven: for so persecuted they the prophets which were before you.

I believe these words that Jesus spoke were meant to encourage and explain to us what we as believers in Jesus Christ will experience in the future. It explains to us what we will experience in Heaven as well as what we will experience on the New Earth.

(Matthew 5:3 KJV)

3. Blessed are the poor in spirit:
for theirs is the kingdom of heaven.

When Jesus says blessed are the poor in spirit for theirs is the kingdom of heaven; He means that those people who desperately know that they can't earn their way to Heaven and that they recognize that only Jesus can save them. By those people admitting that they are spiritually bankrupt in need of a Savior. Jesus says that those people will enter Heaven.

They will enter Heaven not because they trusted in themselves to be saved by their good works but only because they trusted in Jesus Christ to save them and bring them to Heaven.

(Matthew 5:4 KJV)

4. Blessed are they that mourn: for they shall be comforted.

When Jesus said that blessed are those who mourn for they shall be comforted; He meant that even those who mourn about the difficult things in life shall be comforted in the future when they are in Heaven. Whether they are mourning about the death of a loved one, a financial burden, unfortunate circumstances, loneliness, abandonment, or even those who are imprisoned. There are many things that can cause a person to mourn in this life. But Jesus promises us that we shall be comforted. We shall be comforted in Heaven where sadness and sorrow will be gone forever. We can also be comforted right now by reading God's Word and by holding onto God's precious promises. Here is a Bible verse that talks about the comfort that God gives us; so that we can comfort other people who are in need of being comforted as well.

(2 Corinthians 1:3-5 KJV)

3. Blessed be God, even the Father of our Lord Jesus Christ, the Father of mercies, and the God of all comfort; 4. Who comforteth us in all our tribulation, that we may be able to comfort them which are in any trouble, by the comfort wherewith we ourselves are comforted of God. 5. For as the sufferings of Christ abound in us, so our consolation also aboundeth by Christ.

As we are being comforted by God when we go through trials and tribulations each and every day. It is our duty to comfort other people who are going through a similar trial and give them encouragement and hope and tell them to trust God and for them to remember that Jesus Christ will comfort them.

(Matthew 5:5 KJV)

5. Blessed are the meek: for they shall inherit the earth.

When Jesus said blessed are the meek for they shall inherit the earth. He was talking about a specific group of people. As God's children we have incredible power. Now when you think of people being meek you should not think of people as being helpless or weak but a person who is strong. Remember that Jesus was meek but He was definitely not weak. Jesus overturned the money changers tables because he was angry with a righteous anger but he also controlled himself because he made a whip of cords which took a considerable amount of time to make in the first place. Here is the verse.

(John 2:15-17 KJV)

15. And when he had made a scourge of small cords, he drove them all out of the temple, and the sheep, and the oxen; and poured out the changer's money, and overthrew the tables; 16. And said unto them that sold doves, Take these things hence; make not my Father's house an house of merchandise. 17. And his disciples remembered that it was written, The zeal of thine house hath eaten me up.

You see since Jesus is God He saw that the money changers were taking advantage of the true worshippers who came to offer their sacrifices to God. He hated that a lot of these people were offering God their best and the money changers were basically saying that their offering was not good enough. So a lot of those people had to buy their offerings from the money changers. This way of doing things in the temple angered Jesus which is why it says that zeal for thine house hath eaten me up. Jesus was very passionate about the worship of God and for good reason because He is God. My point is that Jesus was in control of His power. Jesus was not out of control He knew exactly what He was doing. A biblical definition of Jesus and meekness; would be power under control. Jesus is power under control. Meekness is power under control. The most powerful being in the universe has His power under control. The most powerful being in the universe has a name and His name is Jesus Christ.

(Matthew 5:5 KJV)

5. Blessed are the meek: for they shall inherit the earth.

When Jesus said blessed are the meek for they shall inherit the earth He had a specific point He was trying to make. Jesus was saying that the people who are meek with one day rule with Jesus Christ on the New Earth. Meek people are to control their power in a godly way to bring honor to their Savior Jesus Christ. Another way to understand meekness is self control. Let's say someone hits you in the face and you are really pumped up and angry. You see the person who hit you and you know you could take that person out because you have incredible strength and power. But you decide to keep that power under control so you walk away from the fight.

That is meekness. Meekness is the ability to know that you have the power to do something but you choose not to do it. Think about when Jesus was being beaten by those Roman soldiers. Jesus had the power to stop it with just one word but He chose not to do so. Or think about when Jesus was on the cross. Jesus could have got off the cross whenever He chose to do so. It was not the nails on the cross that held Jesus there on the cross it was His love for you and me that He decided to die on that cross. And the best part is that three days later He rose from the dead. Now Jesus lives forever in Heaven and He is waiting for you to be with Him forever in Heaven. You will join Him someday if you believe in Jesus Christ and repent of your sins. Repent means to turn away from the bad things you do that you know is wrong. Like when you lie that is a sin. So to repent of the sin of lying is to choose to tell the truth.

(Matthew 5:6 KJV)

6. Blessed are they which do hunger and thirst after
righteousness: for they shall be filled.

When Jesus said blessed are they which do hunger and thirst after righteousness: for they shall be filled; He was making a promise to everyone who desires to live a righteous life. Jesus was saying that people who thirst after righteousness shall be filled in one way. The way that people will be satisfied who thirst after righteousness will be that they will experience righteousness on the New Heavens and New Earth for all of eternity.

Those who desire to see righteousness will one day be overwhelmingly satisfied on the New Heavens and on the New Earth. The New Heavens and the New Earth will become one. They will be united together for all eternity. They will be overjoyed in Heaven and when they are back on the New Earth. They will see all the righteous things that people will do for the glory of God. Think of all the righteous deeds God's people will do towards each other for all of eternity. It will be pure and without any ulterior motives. In Heaven as well on the New Earth people will want to do kind, good, righteous, pure, holy, and wonderful things to one another just because they desire to do them. The main reason for doing them is love. They will want to make each other happy for all of eternity because of the love of Jesus Christ that is in their hearts. Here is a verse that talks about how righteousness will be on the New Heavens and the New Earth.

(2 Peter 3:13 KJV)

13. Nevertheless we, according to his promise, look for new heavens and a new earth, wherein dwelleth righteousness.

Sin will not cover the New Earth. Sin will be gone forever. The only thing that will cover the New Earth will be righteousness. People will desire to please God in all that they do for all of eternity. Their main desire will be to bring glory and honor to Jesus Christ. Whether that is in Heaven or back on the New Earth that desire will be the same. However all of us as Christians and as children of God should desire to bring glory and honor to Jesus Christ while we are still living on this Earth in our daily lives every single day.

(Matthew 5:7 KJV)

7. Blessed are the merciful: for they shall obtain mercy.

When Jesus said blessed are the merciful: for they shall obtain mercy. He was talking about the future judgment of believers in Jesus Christ. He was talking about the Judgment Seat of Christ. When Jesus said blessed are the merciful for they shall obtain mercy I believe Jesus had a specific Bible verse in mind when He looked ahead towards the future. Here is the verse I believe He had in mind.

(James 2:12-13 KJV)

12. So speak ye, and so do, as they that shall be judged by the law of liberty. 13. For he shall have judgment without mercy, that hath shewed no mercy; and mercy rejoiceth against judgment.

If we as believers in Jesus Christ do not show mercy to other people. Then when we are judged by Jesus Christ He will still show us His love for us and He will still forgive us but I believe that He will be disappointed with us. Jesus will have to say things to us, which will be hard for Him to say. It will be extremely hard for us to hear those things spoken by Jesus because we will be filled with regret and remorse because we let Jesus down. Jesus will definitely have to address how we treated other people without mercy. However on the other hand if we are merciful to other people then when we are judged by Jesus Christ; He will show mercy to us and will be proud of what we have done for other people. Jesus will point out every time we showed mercy to people and He will tell us that He was pleased with us.

(Matthew 5:8 KJV)

8. Blessed are the pure in heart: for they shall see God.

When Jesus said blessed are the pure in heart: for they shall see God that was an amazing promise. This promise is amazing because no one has ever seen God before. Here is the verse that talks about no one seeing God before.

(1 John 4:12 KJV)

12. No man hath seen God at any time. If we love one another, God dwelleth in us, and his love is perfected in us.

No one has ever seen God before. There is a verse that many Christians know that says that we can never see God's face. Here is that verse.

(Exodus 33:19-20 KJV)

19. And he said, I will make all my goodness pass before thee, and I will proclaim the name of the Lord before thee; and will be gracious to whom I will be gracious, and will shew mercy on whom I will shew mercy. 20. And he said, Thou canst not see my face: for there shall no man see me, and live.

I do believe that we as sinful people living on a fallen Earth would be dead if we ever saw God's face. However when we as human beings are on the New Earth we will be able to see God's face because we will be clothed with God's Righteousness, which we get only through the blood of Jesus Christ. We will also not be able to sin because in our glorified bodies the temptation to sin will be taken away from us. Our sin nature will be gone. We won't want to sin. We will be disgusted by sin and we will only want to be holy for our Lord and Savior Jesus Christ. Here is a verse explaining that we will have the righteousness of God through Jesus Christ.

(Romans 3:22 KJV)

22. Even the righteousness of God which is by faith of Jesus Christ unto all and upon all them that believe: for there is no difference.

Faith in Jesus Christ and His Blood is what makes us righteous before God.

(Matthew 5:8 KJV)

8. Blessed are the pure in heart: for they shall see God.

When Jesus said blessed are the pure in heart: for they shall see God I believe Jesus was looking forward to the day when on the New Earth we shall see God's face. We shall see God's face on the New Earth. Because we will be clothed in the righteousness of Christ and we will be made sinless. The Bible verse which I believe Jesus had in mind when He said blessed are the pure in heart: for they shall see God; is this verse below.

(Revelation 22:4 KJV)

4. And they shall see his face;
and his name shall be in their foreheads.

This verse in Revelation talks about us seeing God's face and that His name shall be on our foreheads will happen in the future when human beings are living on the New Earth with God Himself. Imagine the awe and beauty of seeing God's face. Then God will also put His name on our foreheads, which in a very real way will label us as belonging to God. Here is the verse about God Himself living with us on the New Earth.

(Revelation 21:3 KJV)

3. And I heard a great voice out of heaven saying, Behold the tabernacle of God is with men, and he will dwell with them, and they shall be his people, and God himself shall be with them, and be their God.

God will live with us on the New Earth. We will have complete access to God.

(Matthew 5:9 KJV)

9. Blessed are the peacemakers:
for they shall be called the children of God.

When Jesus said, blessed are the peacemakers: for they shall be called the children of God. That was an outstanding promise. Jesus is the ultimate peacemaker. Jesus is God. When we act like Jesus we are acting like children of God. When we try to keep the peace or try to create peace in other people we are behaving as children of God. Let's look at some verses about Jesus being the Prince of Peace and the Peace that He gives to us. We all want peace deep down inside but how do we get it? Is there a way to get peace? If there is a way to get peace who do we need to ask in order to find that peace we so deeply crave?

(Isaiah 9:6 KJV)

6. For unto us a child is born, unto us a son is given: and the government shall be upon his shoulder: and his name shall be called Wonderful, Counsellor, The mighty God,
The everlasting Father, The Prince of Peace.

This verse is talking about Jesus Christ. Jesus Christ is Peace. It was a prophecy concerning the birth of Jesus Christ. When Jesus who is God would become a baby. He would grow up and become a man. The God Man. Jesus is the only person who can truly give us the peace that we desire every single day. So what do we have to do in order for Jesus to give us peace? Just ask Jesus for His Peace. Jesus gives us His peace. Look at the words of Jesus that He spoke to us concerning His peace.

(John 14:27 KJV)

27. Peace I leave with you, my peace I give unto you: not as the world giveth, give I unto you. Let not your heart be troubled, neither let it be afraid.

Jesus wants to give us His peace. Jesus is offering His peace to us. All we have to do is ask Jesus for His peace. Let's look at the process of getting the peace of God that Jesus offers us.

(Philippians 4:6-7 KJV)

6. Be careful for nothing; but in every thing by prayer and supplication with thanksgiving let your requests be made known unto God. 7. And the peace of God, which passeth all understanding, shall keep your hearts and minds through Christ Jesus.

The way to be free from anxiety is to not worry about anything. We need to pray to God about everything. We also should thank God for all that He has done for us in the past. If we do these things we shall have a peace because we know that God is trustworthy and faithful to come through for us.

We leave all of our anxieties and fears and lay them down at Jesus Christ's feet. Another way of saying that is found in the book of 1 Peter. Here is the verse.

(1 Peter 5:7 KJV)

7. Casting all your care upon him; for he careth for you.

As we tell God about everything that causes us to have anxiety; we can have confidence that God will take care of it. God will take care of all of our fears and anxieties because He cares for us. Everything that we care about in this world we should tell God about. And trust that He will not let us down. How can Jesus give us the peace that we desire? How do we find inner peace? Well, the only way to find inner peace is to have peace with God. Jesus offers us that peace because He is The Prince of Peace. Jesus is Peace. Let us see how we find peace with God. Here is the verse.

(Romans 5:1 KJV)

1. Therefore being justified by faith, we have peace with God through our Lord Jesus Christ:

And what did Jesus Christ do for us that allowed us to have peace with God? Jesus Christ came down from Heaven and was born as a baby. God put on flesh and became a human being. He then grew up and became a man and lived a sinless life and finally He died on a cross to pay for our sins. But it did not end with His death because three days later Jesus Christ rose from the dead proving that He was God. Now Jesus offers to everyone the forgiveness of their sins and peace with God. Why did Jesus have to die such a painful death? Well the Trinity or the Triune Godhead which consists of God the Father, God the Son, and God the Holy Spirit all decided together that this was the only way to save humankind from their sins and destruction. God came up with a plan to save us from Hell because He never wanted any person to go there. There was no other way for humanity to be saved.

(1 Peter 1:18-20 KJV)

18. Forasmuch as ye know that ye were not redeemed with corruptible things, as silver and gold, from your vain conversation received by tradition from your fathers; 19. But with the precious blood of Christ, as of a lamb without blemish and without spot: 20. Who verily was foreordained before the foundation of the world, but was manifest in these last times for you,

(Revelation 13:8 KJV)

8. And all that dwell upon the earth shall worship him, whose names are not written in the book of life of the Lamb slain from the foundation of the world.

Jesus Christ is the Lamb of God. Jesus is the Lamb that was slaughtered before the world was made. Since God is outside of time He could see Jesus as already sacrificing Himself for our sins. Jesus was the Lamb that was chosen from before the foundation of the world. This was God's plan to save humankind. God's plan was for Jesus Christ to die on a bloody cross to pay for our sins and to rise from the dead three days later. This allowed us to be forgiven so we can be with Jesus in Heaven and then we will come back with Jesus to live with Him on the New Earth.

(John 1:29 KJV)

29. The next day John seeth Jesus coming unto him, and saith, Behold the Lamb of God, which taketh away the sin of the world.

Jesus Christ is the Lamb of God. Jesus takes away the sins of the world. That is how we can be forgiven and accepted by God into Heaven.

(Matthew 5:10 KJV)

10. Blessed are they which are persecuted for righteousness' sake: for theirs is the kingdom of heaven.

When Jesus said, blessed are they, which are persecuted for righteousness' sake: for theirs is the kingdom of heaven. That was a promise but it also probably shocked his disciples. It is difficult to think of yourself as being blessed when you are being persecuted. Whether that is being in jail for your faith, being killed for your faith, or even losing your job for your faith. Yet Jesus says that we are blessed. But notice that Jesus is not saying that at the moment when you are being persecuted that it is a good thing. Jesus is saying it is a good thing when you are being persecuted because as you look ahead into the future you can remind yourself that yours is the kingdom of Heaven.

When Jesus says that theirs is the kingdom of Heaven; Jesus is merely saying that we are citizens of Heaven. Here is a Bible verse about us being citizens of Heaven.

(Philippians 3:20-21 KJV)

20. For our conversation is in heaven; from whence also we look for the Saviour, the Lord Jesus Christ: 21. Who shall change our vile body, that it may be fashioned like unto his glorious body, according to the working whereby he is able even to subdue all things unto himself.

We are citizens of a heavenly country. We long for a paradise city where there will be no pain, no death, no sorrow, and no crying. We desire a city with love, righteousness, justice, fairness, and happiness. God has prepared a heavenly city for the children of God. Here is a Bible verse explaining things that will not be on the New Earth. This is God's promise to us as believers in Jesus Christ. We have this hope if we belong to Jesus Christ.

(Revelation 21:4 KJV)

4. And God shall wipe away all tears from their eyes; and there shall be no more death, neither sorrow, nor crying, neither shall there be any more pain: for the former things are passed away.

Think about a world with no more death. Think about living forever and ever on the New Earth. Think about never being sad again. And think about no more pain. What a powerful and wonderful God we serve. This city is for believers in Jesus Christ. This heavenly city is for the citizens of Heaven. The only way to become a citizen of Heaven is to believe in Jesus Christ, ask for His forgiveness of your sins, and repent of your old sins. In other words leave the old sinful lifestyle behind you. Begin to live a new life in Jesus Christ. Here is a verse that talks about how God has prepared for us a heavenly city.

(Hebrews 11:16 KJV)

16. But now they desire a better country, that is, an heavenly:
wherefore God is not ashamed to be called their God:
for he hath prepared for them a city.

Did you catch that amazing promise? It says that God is not ashamed of us to be called our God. And not only is He not ashamed of us but He has prepared a beautiful, wonderful, awe-inspiring, heavenly city for His children. Whatever you have done, are doing, or will do in the future. Just remember that God is not ashamed of you. He loves you completely and unconditionally. There is nothing you can do that would make Him love you more. And there is nothing you can do that will make Him love you less.

God has an unconditional love for you. Unconditional love means no conditions. In other words God's love for you is not based on your performance or how well you behave. It is based on the pure fact that He loves you because as a believer in Jesus Christ you become a child of God. Think of it this way. A father loves his precious little baby unconditionally. The baby can't do anything to improve the Father's love. The baby can't talk and tell the Father how grateful the baby is for being loved by the Father. The baby can't win awards to make the father love them more. In fact the baby is dependent on everything from the father. The baby needs to eat, drink, sleep, and be washed clean. Even though the baby can't do anything to win the Father's affection. The father loves the baby unconditionally because he finds his happiness and delight in his baby.

In the same way God the Father looks at you and finds happiness and delight in you. God the Father loves you unconditionally and there is nothing you can do to change that. No amount of failures, crimes, lust, pride, hate, or greed can change how much God loves you. Let's make it a little more personal. Jesus loves you. Remember Jesus is God. Jesus sees you where you are at this moment and He loves you. It does not matter the surroundings or circumstances that you are in. If you are a person who is in jail because of your faith in Jesus Christ; then I want you to know that Jesus looks at you and sees a child of God. The world may say that you are worthless and forget about you. But Jesus cares about you. Jesus is with you in that jail cell every single day. If you are a persecuted Christian who is in jail then I would like to remind you that Heaven is your true home. Jesus will give you the Crown of Life for you suffering for His name. Here is the verse.

(Revelation 2:10 KJV)

10. Fear none of those things which thou shalt suffer: behold, the devil shall cast some of you into prison, that ye may be tried; and ye shall have tribulation ten days: be thou faithful unto death, and I will give thee a crown of life.

I would also like to encourage you that if you are a person who is in jail for your faith in Jesus Christ to remember that Jesus Christ was also in jail.

Here is a verse about Jesus telling us that we would suffer persecution because we belong to Him. Persecuted Christian who is in jail let this verse be an encouragement to you. This verse is the words of Jesus speaking to you personally.

(John 15:18-21 KJV)

18. If the world hate you, ye know that it hated me before it hated you. 19. If ye were of the world, the world would love his own: but because ye are not of the world, but I have chosen you out of the world, therefore the world hateth you. 20. Remember the word that I said unto you, The servant is not greater than his lord. If they have persecuted me, they will also persecute you; if they have kept my saying, they will keep yours also. 21. But all these things will they do unto you for my name's sake, because they know not him that sent me.

(Acts 9:5 KJV)

5. And he said, Who art thou, Lord? And the Lord said, I am Jesus whom thou persecutest: it is hard for thee to kick against the pricks.

Jesus knows what it is like to be persecuted. And He is right there with you in the battle every day. If you are being persecuted for your faith just remember that Jesus Christ was persecuted first for you. Jesus experienced rejection for you. Jesus will never abandon you or forsake you. Remember the words of Jesus Christ.

(Matthew 28:19-20 KJV)

19. Go ye therefore, and teach all nations, baptizing them in the name of the Father, and of the Son, and of the Holy Ghost: 20. Teaching them to observe all things whatsoever I have commanded you: and, lo, I am with you always, even unto the end of the world. Amen.

Jesus will always be with you wherever you go. Remember Jesus was condemned as a criminal but Jesus was completely righteous and innocent. Jesus died a criminal's death. If you have been arrested for your faith in Jesus Christ remember that Jesus knows what it's like to be in jail. He knows what you are going through. He knows the thoughts that go through your head every single day. Jesus understands exactly how you feel because He went through the exact same thing.

Here is the verse explaining Jesus Christ being arrested.

(John 18:12 KJV)

12. Then the band and the captain and officers of the Jews took Jesus, and bound him,

If people beat you up in prison and say evil things about you remember that Jesus Christ was also beaten; and people were constantly saying evil things about Him. Here is the verse explaining Jesus Christ being beaten and people saying evil things about Him.

(Luke 22:63-65 KJV)

63. And the men that held Jesus mocked him, and smote him. 64. And when they had blindfolded him, they struck him on the face, and asked him, saying, Prophesy, who is it that smote thee? 65. And many other things blasphemously spake they against him.

Jesus Christ is the one person who truly understands what you are going through each day. You can talk to Him about anything. Jesus is your best friend and Savior that you will ever meet.

(Matthew 5:11-12 KJV)

11. Blessed are ye, when men shall revile you, and persecute you, and shall say all manner of evil against you falsely, for my sake. 12. Rejoice, and be exceeding glad: for great is your reward in heaven: for so persecuted they the prophets which were before you.

When Jesus says blessed are ye, when men shall revile you, and persecute you, and shall say all manner of evil against you falsely, for my sake. Rejoice, and be exceeding glad: for great is your reward in heaven: for so persecuted they the prophets which were before you. Jesus was talking about the great reward in Heaven that you will get because you are being persecuted for Jesus Christ's name. Because you follow Jesus and are a child of God one day you will be rewarded for all you have had to endure for Jesus Christ. You can be confident that Jesus Christ will reward you greatly in Heaven.

God the Father will reward you openly in Heaven. Or in other words God the Father will reward you publicly in Heaven in front of angels and God's people. Here is the verse explaining that. Think about that. God will reward you publicly for the persecution you have went through for His name.

(Matthew 6:3-4 KJV)

3. But when thou doest alms, let not thy left hand know what thy right hand doeth: 4. That thine alms may be in secret: and thy Father which seeth in secret himself shall reward thee openly.

The charitable deeds, which you did in Jesus name in secret to help people in need will not be forgotten. You will be rewarded. In short Heaven and Jesus will be amazing. Heaven will be a beautiful place with a beautiful Savior. We will get to see the One who made everything just by speaking a word from His mouth.

When God said, "Let there be light."

Jesus says in His own words that your reward in Heaven will be great. If a reward in Heaven is beyond anything we can imagine; then think about how amazing it will be when we receive a great reward in Heaven? The best part is that Jesus is the One who will be rewarding us personally in front of everyone in Heaven.

I care about your soul and I want to see you in Heaven. But more importantly Jesus Christ wants to see you in Heaven with Him. Jesus wants to see you in Heaven with Him so much that He went and died on a bloody cross 2,000 years ago for you. He died to pay for your sins and He rose from the dead so that you can be justified in the sight of God.

In other words when God sees you; He sees you covered by the blood of His Son Jesus Christ. God sees you in a right standing with Him. Or to break it down even more simple. When God looks at you He does not see your sins anymore. God sees the Righteousness of Jesus Christ. If you are not a Christian, a believer in Jesus Christ, a child of God, or if you are not saved then I would like to encourage you and plead with you to pray this prayer. If you don't get saved you will never be able to experience all the goodness of Jesus and the beauty of Heaven. That would break God's heart. Here is the prayer.

Dear Jesus I know that I'm a sinner. I know that there is nothing I can do to earn your forgiveness. I also know that I deserve to go to Hell. But thank you Jesus for dieing for me on the cross 2,000 years ago. I ask for your forgiveness Lord Jesus. Please forgive me Jesus of all of my sins. I want to go to Heaven to be with you forever Jesus. Please come into my life and change me Jesus. I repent and turn away from my life of sin. Thank you for loving me Jesus so much that you were willing to die for me to save me from Hell. I want to start this eternal relationship with you Jesus right now. Jesus please help me to serve you all the days of my life from this day forward. I love you Jesus. I pray this in Jesus name.

Amen.